✧   *Companions for the Journey*   ✧

# Praying with
# Mother Teresa

*✧ Companions for the Journey ✧*

# Praying with
# Mother Teresa

by
**Jean Maalouf**

**Saint Mary's Press**
**Christian Brothers Publications**
**Winona, Minnesota**

✧  *To my dear family and friends*  ✧
*and especially to my sister*
*who has always been inspired*
*by Saint Thérèse of Lisieux*
*and Mother Teresa of Calcutta*

 Genuine recycled paper with 10% post-consumer waste.
Printed with soy-based ink.

The publishing team for this book included Cheryl Drivdahl, manuscript editor; James H. Gurley, production editor and typesetter; Cären Yang, cover designer; Sam Thiewes, illustrator; produced by the graphics division of Saint Mary's Press.

The acknowledgments continue on page 129.

Printed in the United States of America

Printing: 9 8 7 6 5 4 3 2 1

Year: 2008 07 06 05 04 03 02 01 00

ISBN 0-88489-640-4


Library of Congress Cataloging-in-Publication Data

Maalouf, Jean.
    Praying with Mother Teresa / by Jean Maalouf.
        p. cm. — (Companions for the journey)
Includes bibliographical references.
    ISBN 0-88489-640-4 (pbk. : alk. paper)
1. Teresa, Mother, 1910– 2. Catholic Church—Prayer-books and devotions—
English. I. Title. II. Series.
    BX4406.5.Z8 M22 2000
    242—dc21
                                99-050865

# ✧ Contents ✧

Series Foreword     7

Introduction     13

Meditations

  1. **Life in Christ**     30

  2. **The Urgency of Prayer**     35

  3. **Silence**     41

  4. **Love at the Center**     47

  5. **Minding the Call**     53

  6. **A Life for the Poor**     59

  7. **Contemplation in the Heart of the World**     66

  8. **The Secret of Joy**     73

  9. **Trust in God**     80

10. **Family Life**     87

11. **Leadership**     95

12. **Peacemaking**     102

13. **Instrumentality**     107

14. **Devotion to Mary**     113

15. **Holiness Is for You and Me**     120

Works Cited     126

For Further Reading     128

# ✧ Series Foreword ✧

## Companions for the Journey

Just as food is required for human life, so are companions. Indeed, the word *companions* comes from two Latin words: *com*, meaning "with," and *panis*, meaning "bread." Companions nourish our heart, mind, soul, and body. They are also the people with whom we can celebrate the sharing of bread.

Perhaps the most touching stories in the Bible are about companionship: the Last Supper, the wedding feast at Cana, the sharing of the loaves and the fishes, and Jesus' breaking of bread with the disciples on the road to Emmaus. Each incident of companionship with Jesus revealed more about his mercy, love, wisdom, suffering, and hope. When Jesus went to pray in the Garden of Olives, he craved the companionship of the Apostles. They let him down. But God sent the Spirit to inflame the hearts of the Apostles, and they became faithful companions to Jesus and to one another.

Throughout history, other faithful companions have followed Jesus and the Apostles. These saints and mystics have also taken the journey from conversion, through suffering, to resurrection. Just as they were inspired by the holy people who went before them, so too may you be inspired by these saints and mystics and take them as your companions on your spiritual journey.

The Companions for the Journey series is a response to the spiritual hunger of Christians. This series makes available the rich spiritual teachings of mystics and guides whose wisdom can help us on our pilgrimage. As you complete the last meditation in each volume, it is hoped that you will feel supported, challenged, and affirmed by a soul-companion on your spiritual journey.

The spiritual hunger that has emerged over the last twenty years is a great sign of renewal in Christian life. People fill retreat programs and workshops on topics in spirituality. The demand for spiritual directors exceeds the number available. Interest in the lives and writings of saints and mystics is increasing as people search for models of whole and holy Christian life.

# Praying with Mother Teresa

*Praying with Mother Teresa* is more than just a book about the spirituality of Mother Teresa of Calcutta. This book seeks to engage you in praying in the way that Mother Teresa did about issues and themes that were central to her experience. Each meditation can enlighten your understanding of her spirituality and lead you to reflect on your own experience.

The goal of *Praying with Mother Teresa* is that you will discover Mother Teresa's rich spirituality and integrate her spirit and wisdom into your relationship with God, with your brothers and sisters, and with your own heart and mind.

## Suggestions for Praying with Mother Teresa

Meet Mother Teresa, a fascinating companion for your pilgrimage, by reading the introduction to this book. It provides a brief biography of Mother Teresa and an outline of the major themes of her spirituality.

Once you meet Mother Teresa, you will be ready to pray with her and to encounter God, your sisters and brothers, and yourself in new and wonderful ways. To help your prayer, here are some suggestions that have been part of the tradition of Christian spirituality:

**Create a sacred space.** Jesus said, "Whenever you pray, go into your room and shut the door and pray to your [God] who is in secret; and your [God] who sees in secret will reward you" (Matthew 6:6). Solitary prayer is best done in a place where you can have privacy and silence, both of which can be luxuries in the life of busy people. If privacy and silence are not possible, create a quiet, safe place within yourself, perhaps while riding to and from work, while sitting in line at the dentist's office, or while waiting for someone. Do the best you can, knowing that a loving God is present everywhere. Whether the meditations in this book are used for solitary prayer or with a group, try to create a prayerful mood with candles, meditative music, an open Bible, or a crucifix.

**Open yourself to the power of prayer.** Every human experience has a religious dimension. All of life is suffused with God's presence. So remind yourself that God is present as you begin your period of prayer. Do not worry about distractions. If something keeps intruding during your prayer, spend some time talking with God about it. Be flexible because God's spirit blows where it will.

Prayer can open your mind and widen your vision. Be open to new ways of seeing God, people, and yourself. As you open yourself to the spirit of God, different emotions are evoked, such as sadness from tender memories, or joy from a celebration recalled. Our emotions are messages from God that can tell us much about our spiritual quest. Also, prayer strengthens our will to act. Through prayer, God can touch our will and empower us to live according to what we know is true.

Finally, many of the meditations in this book will call you to employ your memories, your imagination, and the circumstances of your life as subjects for prayer. The great mystics and saints realized that they had to use all their resources to know God better. Indeed, God speaks to us continually and touches us constantly. We must learn to listen and feel with all the means that God has given us.

Come to prayer with an open mind, heart, and will.

**Preview each meditation before beginning.** After you have placed yourself in God's presence, spend a few moments previewing the readings and especially the reflection activities. Several reflection activities are given in each meditation because different styles of prayer appeal to different personalities or personal needs. **Note that each meditation has more reflection activities than can be done during one prayer period. Therefore, select only one or two reflection activities each time you use a meditation. Do not feel compelled to complete all the reflection activities.**

**Read meditatively.** Each meditation offers you a story about Mother Teresa and one or more readings from her writings. Take your time reading. If a particular phrase touches you, stay with it. Relish its feelings, meanings, and concerns.

**Use the reflections.** Following the readings is a short reflection in commentary form, which is meant to give perspective to the readings. Then you are offered several ways of meditating on the readings and the theme of the prayer. You may be familiar with the different methods of meditating, but in case you are not, they are described briefly here:

✦ *Repeated short prayer or mantra:* One means of focusing your prayer is to use a *mantra,* or "prayer word." The mantra may be a single word or a short phrase taken from the readings or from the Scriptures. For example, a short prayer for meditation 4 in this book might simply be "Jesus loves me." Repeated slowly in harmony with your breathing, the mantra helps you center your heart and mind on one action or attribute of God.

✦ *Lectio divina:* This type of meditation is "divine studying," a concentrated reflection on the word of God or the wisdom of a spiritual writer. Most often in *lectio divina,* you will be invited to read a passage several times and then concentrate on one or two sentences, pondering their meaning for you and their effect on you. *Lectio divina* commonly ends with formulation of a resolution.

✦ *Guided meditation:* In this type of meditation, our imagination helps us consider alternative actions and likely consequences. Our imagination helps us experience new ways of seeing God, our neighbors, ourselves, and nature. When Jesus told his followers parables and stories, he engaged their imagination. In this book, you will be invited to follow a guided meditation.

One way of doing a guided meditation is to read the scene or story several times, until you know the outline and can recall it when you enter into reflection. Or before your prayer time, you may wish to record the meditation on a tape recorder. If so, remember to allow pauses for reflection between phrases and to speak with a slow, peaceful pace and tone. Then, during prayer, when you have finished the readings and the reflection commentary, you can turn on your recording of the meditation and be led through it. If you find your own voice too distracting, ask a friend to make the tape for you.

✦ *Examen of consciousness:* The reflections often will ask you to examine how God has been speaking to you in your past and present experience—in other words, the reflections will ask you to examine your awareness of God's presence in your life.

✦ *Journal writing:* Writing is a process of discovery. If you write for any length of time, stating honestly what is on your mind and in your heart, you will unearth much about who you are, how you stand with your God, what deep longings reside in your soul, and more. For some reflections, you may wish to write a dialogue with Jesus or someone else. If you have never used writing as a means of meditation, try it. Reserve a special notebook for your journal writing. If desired, you can go back to your entries at a future time for an examen of consciousness.

✦ *Action:* Occasionally, a reflection will suggest singing a favorite hymn, going out for a walk, or undertaking some other physical activity. Actions can be meaningful forms of prayer.

## Using the Meditations for Group Prayer

If you wish to use the meditations for community prayer, these suggestions may help:

✦ Read the theme to the group. Call the community into the presence of God, using the short opening prayer. Invite one or two participants to read one or both readings on Mother Teresa. If you use both readings, observe the pause between them.

✦ The reflection commentary may be used as a reading, or it may be deleted, depending on the needs and interests of the group.

✦ Select one of the reflection activities for your group. Allow sufficient time for your group to reflect, to recite a centering prayer or mantra, to accomplish a studying prayer *(lectio divina)*, or to finish an examen of consciousness. Depending on the group and the amount of available time, you may want to invite the participants to share their reflections, responses, or petitions with the group.

✦ Reading the words from the Scriptures may serve as a summary of the meditation.

✦ If a formulated prayer or a psalm is given as a closing, it may be recited by the entire group. Or you may ask participants to offer their own prayers for the closing.

Now you are ready to begin praying with Mother Teresa, a faithful and caring companion on this stage of your spiritual journey. It is hoped that you will find her to be a true soul-companion.

# ✧ Introduction ✧

## Mother Teresa of Calcutta: A Woman in Love

The story of Mother Teresa—who has been called the most revered and the most powerful woman in the world—is simply an extraordinary love story. Jesus Christ was her beloved, her main focus, and was at the very center of her entire life.

Mother Teresa lived in God's presence as much as a human being can. She lived a contemplative life in the world of action. She was the uncompromising lover of her God and of all human beings in whom God dwells, especially the poorest of the poor. She showed by her words, and especially by her example, that holiness is available to, possible for, and even imperative to everyone. She was genuine. No wonder many people believed her to be a living saint and an event in the history of the faith journey.

## Born and Called to a Life in Christ

Mother Teresa was born Agnes Gonxha Bojaxhiu in 1910 in Skopje, Albania. She was the third and last child of Nikolle Bojaxhiu and Drana Bernai. Her parents, especially her mother, were devout Catholics. Agnes's father died when she was only nine years old. She said of her childhood and adolescence: "We were all very united, especially after the death of my father. We lived for each other and we made every effort to make one another happy. We were a very united and a very happy family" (Neff, p. 34).

Lazar, Agnes's brother, commented: "We lived next to the parish church of the Sacred Heart of Jesus. Sometimes my mother and sisters seemed to live as much in the church as they did at home. They were always involved with the choir, the religious services, and missionary topics" (Mother Teresa, *No Greater Love*, pp. 191–192).

Their mother never allowed any poor people to go empty-handed. "Keep in mind," she would say to her children, "that even those who are not our blood relatives, even if they are poor, are still our brethren" (p. 192).

At the age of twelve, Agnes started to feel called to a religious and missionary life. In 1927, she discovered her vocation before the altar of the Patroness of Skopje. "Our Lady," she said many years later, "interceded for me and helped me to discover my vocation" (p. 193).

At the age of eighteen, Agnes felt a strong desire to join the Sisters of Our Lady of Loreto (commonly called the Irish Ladies), a group of nuns who worked in India. Her mother was shocked by the decision, but her parish priest was not surprised. Though her family at first reacted with disbelief and frustration, they eventually encouraged her to go wherever God was leading her.

In 1928, Agnes, weeping, waved good-bye to her family and boarded a train for the first leg of her journey to the Loreto Abbey in Dublin, Ireland, where she was to study English. About two months later, her English was deemed good enough for her to travel to India, where she would start her novitiate (a period of study and contemplation required before taking vows to be a nun).

In the foothills of the Himalayas, at the Loreto sisters' convent in Darjeeling, Agnes began her novitiate in 1929. She studied the Scriptures, the rules of the Loreto order, more English, and the Indian languages of Hindi and Bengali. She also practiced the arts of meditation and silence.

On 24 May 1931, Agnes vowed to commit herself to poverty, chastity, and obedience. She chose the name Sister Teresa, after Saint Thérèse of Lisieux (of the child Jesus), the patron saint of missionaries, whose vocation was love. Agnes took this name because Saint Thérèse wrote in her *Story of a Soul*, "Love contains all vocations." Agnes was convinced, as Saint Thérèse had been, that she could live a life of goodness, simplicity, spiritual childhood, a complete self-surrender to God's will, and the love that contains all vocations.

Sister Teresa's first assignment was to teach geography and history in the convent school at Entally, a district of Calcutta. She also taught younger students at Saint Mary's School. She described her life with these words: "I was the happiest nun at Loreto. I dedicated myself to teaching. That job, carried out for the love of God, was a true apostolate. I liked it very much" (Neff, p. 36). Sister Marie-Thérèse Breen, who was with her in the Darjeeling novitiate and for several years after, had this to say about her in that period:

[Sister Teresa was always very simple and very nice. . . . There was nothing extraordinary about her. Just that she was a very simple, ordinary girl. Very gentle, full of fun. Enjoyed everything that went on. . . .

. . . She was a very hard worker. . . . Up to time on this, up to time on that. She never wanted to shirk anything, she was always ready. Always a very pious person, she was just herself. She did not force it on anybody, if you like, she was just what she felt she had to be. . . . She fitted in very well; we were all very happy, very happy. (Chawla, pp. 11–12)

On 14 May 1937, Sister Teresa took her final vows, promising to serve God for the rest of her life.

Afterward, Sister Teresa continued teaching at Entally and eventually became principal there. Though the school's buildings were somewhat isolated from the poverty of the surrounding area, Sister Teresa saw the slum and witnessed the suffering of its inhabitants. She began to ask herself whether she was doing God's will. But she could not go out to help; the order's rule of enclosure prohibited a nun from leaving the convent unless she needed hospital care or went to the annual retreat at Darjeeling.

For nearly twenty years, Sister Teresa lived as a Loreto nun and strictly followed the rules and schedules of the Loreto order. Then, on 10 September 1946, something changed her life—and the history of Christianity—forever. This was her "day of inspiration." While praying in a train going from Calcutta to Darjeeling, she felt, she said, a call within her calling.

She understood clearly that she had to consecrate her life to the poorest of the poor.

Two years later, she obtained permission from Rome to pursue her new calling. On 16 August 1948, she put on a white sari instead of the religious habit of the Sisters of Our Lady of Loreto, and left the convent to fulfill her new mission. Later, she said that parting from Loreto was harder than saying good-bye to her family and her country.

Sister Teresa's first steps outside the order she loved took her to Patna, north of Calcutta. She felt, and was also advised, that she needed basic training in medical first aid and nursing care. The Medical Missionary Sisters, who provide medical service for the poor, helped her to acquire that training. In the approximately three months she spent with them, Sister Teresa became more aware of important nutrition and hygiene principles, and she learned to give injections, prescribe medicines, and manage a medical facility.

In December 1948, Sister Teresa returned to Calcutta. She stayed temporarily with the Little Sisters of the Poor, a Catholic order that runs the Saint Joseph's Home for older people. Just a few days later, she felt ready to begin her work at the Motijhil slums, which are located about an hour away. She walked alone, looking for little ways to help, with no specific plans for what to do. She started with what was familiar to her: she asked a few Motijhil families if she could teach their children. Under a tree, she taught them, along with the alphabet, personal hygiene. Then she started to visit her students' families. She helped them clean their homes and clothes. She gave them her time and energy. Especially, she gave them her great love.

In the beginning, Sister Teresa's new calling was not easy. Not everyone in Motijhil was happy with her. Even though many residents gratefully supported her efforts, many others, suspecting that she was just trying to convert them to Christianity, asked her to leave. She had no permanent home, and she experienced moments of loneliness, anguish, and exhaustion. At times she was tempted by the memory of her happy life as a Loreto sister; then she would pray to God:

My God, I choose freely
    and because I love you,
I choose to remain faithful to my decision,
    and to do only your will.

(Egan, At Prayer, p. 63)

Her vision was so great that she was ready to overcome every difficulty. Eileen Egan, who knew her for a long time and traveled with her extensively, says:

> She seemed to have no needs of her own, but to be ready to respond to any need around her, ready to be a channel

of healing to those who came to her almost inconsolable in their sorrow. . . . No matter how great the commotion around her, Mother Teresa seemed to be at rest, her mind and heart centered on Jesus. (Pp. 16–17)

Inflamed by her calling and her new vision, Sister Teresa continued to help and serve the poor. Soon, one large donation allowed her to rent two rooms that became her schoolrooms and small medical facility.

A few months later, the number of her students increased, volunteer teachers appeared, and more donations were sent. She was now able to direct new efforts to another slum district, not far from Motijhil. Another school was created. Sister Teresa started to feel the need for a home closer to the slums. She found a room in the house of an Indian Catholic family that gave her strong support.

Her mission in the slums continued to grow:

One by one, [she said,] I saw young girls arrive after 1949.
They were my students. They wanted to give everything to God, and they were in a hurry to do so. (Mother Teresa, *My Life*, pp. 11–12)

In 1950, she founded the Order of the Missionaries of Charity and became officially Mother Superior, better known as Mother Teresa—a title some people had been using since she had become principal of Saint Mary's School in 1937.

Her new order expanded day after day, until Mother Teresa felt the need for larger headquarters. She and her sisters prayed intensely and persistently for this. The answer to their prayers came when a man led Mother Teresa to a three-story building at Lower Circular Road. The owner of the building, who was a Muslim, sold it to Mother Teresa for a fraction of its real value, as a contributory gesture for the good work she was doing.

In 1953, the nearly thirty Missionaries of Charity had an official motherhouse at 54 A Lower Circular Road. Air conditioners, electric fans, washing machines, and any other modern comforts were not allowed there. The sisters wanted to be in every way like the poor they served. They accepted only what people gave them. Each sister owned usually three saris, one pair of sandals, and virtually nothing else. God was their provider. They believed that if God wanted this order, God would provide the means to accomplish its ends.

In 1969, the Co-Workers of the Missionaries of Charity, a group of laymen and laywomen, was officially affiliated with the Missionaries of Charity.

With Mother Teresa's leadership, the Missionaries of Charity and the Co-Workers continued to expand in number and charitable activities. Over the years, they have spread their work to more than one hundred countries. They have formed a large network of schools, of dispensaries, and of homes for mentally handicapped people and abandoned children and lepers, for alcoholics and drug addicts, for the destitute and dying, and for unwed mothers. They have provided daily cooked food and emergency relief. Also, they have created centers for those suffering from malnutrition, tuberculosis, and AIDS.

As Mother Teresa and her followers gained international recognition, journalists became eager to know more about her and her mystery. To their curiosity, her answer was that she had a happy childhood and a happy religious life. Then she switched the conversation to the poor, and how the poor should be helped. Even when her health started to deteriorate in 1988–89, even when she was hospitalized for chest pains and doctors and others were willing to make every effort to save her, she remained calm, ready to die without fanfare, like the poor she served. She never wanted to admit, even during the years when her health failed, that the word *fragile* could apply to her. She just wanted to continue to work as she had always done.

On 5 September 1997, at the age of eighty-seven, Mother Teresa died. Her three-hour state funeral was partly a Roman Catholic rite and partly a memorial service addressed by leaders from other faiths and by representatives from foreign governments.

"[Mother Teresa] learned to see the face of God in every suffering human being," said Angelo Cardinal Sodano, the Vatican secretary of state, in a eulogy delivered on behalf of Pope John Paul II. He added, "[Mother Teresa,] the entire church thanks you for your luminous example and promises to make it our heritage," and he said: "I thank you for all you have done for the poor of the world. Dear Mother Teresa, rest in peace" (Crossette, p. 14).

## Unconditional Love

The only language that God understands is the language of love. God loves and wants to be loved. God says, "You are my beloved." But God also asks: "Do you love me? Do you really love me?" We have countless opportunities to answer yes or no.

All our spiritual life depends on the yes we say to God; after it, our entire life changes radically. Being here or there, pursuing a career or not, being praised and showered with awards or harshly rejected, walking or resting, having money or nothing, living or dying—whatever we are and have and do, however we live, becomes our answer to that inviting and demanding question, "Do you love me?"

Mother Teresa answered unambiguously a passionate yes. She said it in words. She said it with her life, living those words.

Of course she was interested in the fruition of her work. She founded a religious order, and then a lay group to support it. She built, throughout the world, hundreds of centers, clinics, houses, and shelters for people in need, and daily cooked for alcoholics and drug addicts, mentally handicapped and abandoned children, unwed mothers, dying destitutes, and so on. But all this—even though extraordinary—was not the point. Her deepest concerns were the questions, "Am I in love with Jesus Christ?" and then "Am I in love with the incarnate God who identified with the sick, the imprisoned, the outcast, the lonely, the abandoned, the dying?" Her earnest yes to these questions allowed her to give sense to all that she had done throughout the world.

Mother Teresa said:

The Missionaries of Charity are not social activists but contemplatives in the very heart of today's world. We take literally the words of Jesus: "I was hungry, I was naked, without a home, and you gave me food, you clothed me, you gave me shelter" (see Mt 25:35–36). In this way we are in contact with him twenty-four hours a day. This contemplation, this touching of Christ in the poor, is beautiful, very real, and full of love. (Mother Teresa, *Heart of Joy*, p. 32)

Indeed, Mother Teresa's philosophy of life was based on the reality of the Incarnation, the heart of God becoming "a heart of flesh" in Jesus. She truly believed that knowing and living God's heart means proclaiming that "God is love" (1 John 4:8) and only love. She also understood that "we love because [God] first loved us" (1 John 4:19).

Jesus Christ, the encounter of the love of God, cries out loudly, "Let anyone who is thirsty come to me, and let the one who believes in me drink" (John 7:37). He says: "Come to me, all you that are weary and are carrying heavy burdens, and I will give you rest. Take my yoke upon you, and learn from me; for I am gentle and humble in heart, and you will find rest for your souls" (Matthew 11:28–29). Mother Teresa's unconditional love for this Jesus Christ was the true secret behind and real motivation for what she did. Her leadership was rooted in an intimate relationship with the incarnate Jesus, and Jesus Christ was the source of her inspiration and guidance, her very breath. That is why her success was certain and great. That is why she was capable of inspiring new life and hope, bringing healing and awareness, and spreading love and reconciliation. And that is why she could be convinced without being fanatical, be flexible without being relativistic, be peaceful and kind without being soft and malleable, be willing to confront with kindness without offending others, be tolerant without compromising the truth, attract people to her beliefs without manipulating them, be demanding without being narrow-minded, be scrupulously honest without pestering, and be passionate without being too annoying.

In an intimate and loving relationship with Jesus Christ, over time, the desire to be successful and relevant will seem to matter less and less and will yield to the desire to serve all our brothers and sisters—no matter who, what, or where they are—in the name of the One who said, "Truly I tell you, just as you did it to one of the least of these who are members of my family, you did it to me" (Matthew 25:40). Mother Teresa took Jesus at his word and did exactly what he told her to do. She was in love with Jesus Christ, her Lord, and she saw him and adored him in every woman and man she met and served.

## Peace in Action

What could a nun as simple and poor as Mother Teresa say about world peace? A great deal. Indeed, she was an authentic and inspiring peacemaker.

Through her focus on God's love, Mother Teresa lived peace. Her life itself showed that peace is possible: one can see it and touch it. Although she did not invent a system for establishing world peace, the model of her life is more effective than any sophisticated system that the most creative philosophers and ideologists have come up with. It is no wonder that she was awarded the Nobel Peace Prize, the Soviet Peace Committee Gold Medal, and the Pope John XXIII Peace Prize.

It is no wonder that she dared to write to Presidents George Bush of the United States and Saddam Hussein of Iraq in 1991, in the hope of convincing them not to go to war.

It is no wonder that Pope John Paul II, recognizing her charisma and holiness, chose her to become a trusted collaborator and an ambassadress-at-large.

It is no wonder that she traveled to Assisi in 1986 when the pope asked her to go there and take an active part in a world prayer meeting for peace that gathered spiritual leaders from all religions, nations, languages, and cultures. On the day of that meeting, no one, it seemed, had more right to be at Assisi, or more joy in being there, than Mother Teresa. On leaving Assisi, the participants in the World Prayer Day for Peace repeated one of Mother Teresa's favorite prayers, inspired by Saint Francis, asking God to make them instruments of divine peace.

Mother Teresa did not waste time analyzing and speculating over the existence and the causes of world violence. She did not even strive to change unjust laws, prejudiced conditions, unjustified structures, and partial traditions. No. She filled the human need she saw. She provided food for the hungry. She took care of the sick. She helped the dying to recover or to die with dignity. She touched the hearts of people with her love. She was convinced that the people she served, moved and transformed by love, would have within themselves the capacity to change their own condition and the condition of their own wounded society.

Mother Teresa had it right. Peace stems not from external changes but from a change of heart. Once that internal change takes place, then laws, conditions, structures, and traditions will fall in line to carry out the process of peace. Examples of living truth, like Mother Teresa herself, are often the best teachers of all.

Mother Teresa lived the love, joy, and peace of her Lord—the way to world peace. Her work of love was a concrete example of living peace and making peace. What she said through that work was in substance quite simple: be living peace with your spouse, children, relatives, friends, and community, and care for everyone you meet. Speeches will not bring peace to the world. Small acts of loving-kindness will bring peace—peace in action. Her enormous success demonstrates that this is true, and that through loving actions, everyone, in one way or another, can make a difference in the process of peace.

## An Avalanche of Awards

A life totally devoted to God can be full of paradoxes. Who would think that a genuine and humble nun who had never sought the limelight would be showered with honors and public recognition? Everyone, it seems, was interested in awarding and supporting this unselfish woman. People trusted and admired her complete detachment from earthly goods. Her unconditional love, like a magnet, drew the attention of others and involved them in her cause. Her order spread to every continent, and her worldwide influence brought her a broad range of honors.

In 1962, Mother Teresa was honored with the Padma Sri (Order of the Lotus), a high award given by the government of India. In the same year, in Manila, she was awarded the

Magsaysay Prize by the Conference of Asiatic States and was described as the most worthy woman in Asia.

In 1970, she received the Good Samaritan Prize and the Kennedy Foundation Prize, in the United States.

In 1971, she received the Pope John XXIII Peace Prize at the Vatican.

In 1972, she was awarded the Pandit Nehry Award for International Understanding.

In 1973, she received the Templeton Prize in London and the Saint Louise de Marillac in Los Angeles.

In 1975, she received the Albert Schweitzer Award in the United States.

In 1977, she received an honorary doctorate from Cambridge University in England.

In 1979, she received the Balzan Award from the president of the Italian Republic. Also in that year, she received the most famous international award, the Nobel Peace Prize, in the name of the poor.

In 1985, she received the Presidential Medal of Honor from President Ronald Reagan of the United States.

In 1987, she received the Soviet Peace Committee Gold Medal for promoting peace and friendship between people.

In 1990, she received the International Leo Tolstoy Medal, given by the Soviet government.

In 1992, she received the Peace Education Prize from the United Nations Educational, Scientific, and Cultural Organization (UNESCO). In the same year, she also received the Gaudium et Spes (Joy and Hope) Award from the Knights of Columbus.

In 1996, President Bill Clinton of the United States signed legislation making Mother Teresa an honorary U.S. citizen. Then President Clinton praised Mother Teresa for bringing hope and love to orphaned and abandoned children all over the world.

Probably no one has received so many honors. Somehow, the more reluctant Mother Teresa was to receive any awards, the more she was given. She was a perfect living example for the paradox The more you give away, the more you receive back. When Mother Teresa received anything, she did it for her poor—Christ's poor. Every bit of help then was welcomed, and it was quickly directed to build one more house to welcome and honor Jesus Christ, here and now.

Awards did not spoil Mother Teresa. Rather, they raised people's consciousness and their awareness of her cause.

## Central Themes in Mother Teresa's Spirituality

At the Nobel Prize ceremony in Oslo in 1979, a journalist asked Mother Teresa about her identity. She replied: "By blood and origin, I am Albanian. My citizenship is Indian. I am a Catholic nun. As to my calling, I belong to the whole world. As to my heart, I belong entirely to the heart of Jesus" (Egan, *Such a Vision,* p. 357). These conditions also define her spiritual identity.

Mother Teresa's religion was not just a mental exercise in belief and speculation. She was not a great writer or theologian or philosopher. She was a person of immense compassion, sensitivity, and openness. She was genuine. Her faith was integrated with her compassion, and her compassion dictated her behavior. Her religion was contemplation in action. She did not seek to convert people to her beliefs. She simply lived her beliefs passionately and earnestly, demonstrating that when given the love, kindness, and attention they need, human beings—no matter who and what they are, even if they are the poorest of the poor—are transformed and discover the dignity of being human. She showed us that people are both human and divine. This is why she caught the imagination of the world.

**Living in Christ.** Identification with Christ was the focus of Mother Teresa's life. Her devotion to the poor and needy reflected her understanding that Christ was in her, and that she was in Christ.

**Unlimited confidence in prayer and silence.** "Prayer," according to Mother Teresa, "feeds the soul—as blood is to the body, prayer is to the soul—and it brings you closer to God." She also said, "I always begin my prayer in silence, for it is in the silence of the heart that God speaks" (Mother Teresa, *A Simple Path*, p. 7).

**Unconditional love for Jesus Christ.** Mother Teresa's spirituality centered on her uncompromising passion for her Lord. Through her prayers and works, we see her total commitment to Jesus Christ and the poor who represent him. She saw Jesus Christ in the poor. She loved God and creation. She lived the Gospel with her whole soul, heart, mind, and strength, conscientiously and truthfully. She was a living example for incarnational spirituality.

**Minding God's call.** Mother Teresa believed completely that God had called her to be a nun, and that God had further called her to serve poor people. She was convinced that happiness came from fulfilling the role that God had called her to.

**Boundless compassion for the poor.** The entire world has recognized Mother Teresa's caring for the sick, the poor, and the dying. She showed her deepest compassion and concern for anyone in need. She also extended her definition of the poor to include people who are unwanted, rejected, and unloved—those, she said, are even poorer than the ones who just do not have money. Mother Teresa demonstrated a great sensitivity to spiritual and psychological needs, as well as physical needs.

**Contemplation in the world.** Contemplation and action were not two separate and exclusive concepts to Mother Teresa. She viewed both as faith in action.

**Unceasing joy.** Mother Teresa emphasized the importance of joy in her life and in the lives of her followers, saying, "Joy is prayer; joy is strength; joy is love" (Mother Teresa, *Jesus*, p. 127). Joy is presented in the Rule of the Missionaries of Charity as a gift of the Holy Spirit and a sign of the Reign of God. That is how important it is.

**Unconditional trust in God's providence.** Mother Teresa's life seemed a response to the overwhelming presence of the Divine Love, alive in her entire being. In her philosophy of life and her actions, she counted on Providence for her every need. She trusted that God is the real provider. She worried not.

**Family life.** According to Mother Teresa, family life should be united, peaceful, and holy. She urged all people to make their home like Nazareth, a place where they could invite Jesus Christ to live with them.

**Leadership.** Mother Teresa believed that it is everyone's responsibility to lead others by allowing God to speak through them and by living out God's word.

**Peacemaking.** The closer we live to Jesus Christ, the closer we come to experiencing peace. Mother Teresa's life of peace in Christ gave all people a model for finding peace in their family and in the world.

**Instrumentality.** Total surrender to God was a goal for Mother Teresa. She described herself as a pencil, writing what God desired.

**Devotion to Mary.** For Mother Teresa, loving and trusting Mary is one way to strengthen our relationship with Jesus.

**Holiness and an uncompromising lifestyle.** Mother Teresa's path was total adherence to the teachings of Jesus Christ through poverty and simplicity. Her aim was holiness, which was, in her view, a necessity of life available to everyone.

## Praying with Mother Teresa

"My secret is quite simple," Mother Teresa said: "I pray and through my prayer I become one in love with Christ, and see that praying to him is to love him, and that means to fulfill his words" (Mother Teresa, *Life in the Spirit*, p. 1). Mother Teresa believed in the power of prayer. She believed that God listened to her prayers and the prayers of her sisters. Her trust in God enabled her to obtain what she wanted. She relied completely on the Almighty. She would say: "I take Jesus at his word—he said 'ask and you will receive.' So I ask. If it is for his glory he will grant it; if not, let us forget about it. God knows what is good for us" (Le Joly, *Mother Teresa*, pp. 119–120). Mother Teresa succeeded well because prayer always came first in her life.

## Mother Teresa for Today

People all over the world, from different religious backgrounds, beliefs, races, and nationalities, praise this Catholic nun who everywhere radiated love, service, peace, integrity, and holiness. This amazing person was able to attract men and women, old and young, rich and poor, educated and noneducated, to her Missionaries of Charity and her Co-Workers. She was, for many people, a magnet as well as a challenge. In following her radical steps, those people found meaning for their lives, and happiness through serving others. They discovered the essential and existential satisfaction they were looking for and had never been able to find before.

Mother Teresa was a living answer for every mind and heart that cannot find meaning in greed, anger, hatred, and indifference. Her way of life tells us that there is much more to our journey on earth than acquiring personal possessions. She provided a contemporary model for the qualities of holiness: uncompromising love for God and for others; caring service for those who are poor, sick, and dying; and peacemaking. She showed concretely how to attain all those things. We can certainly trust her companionship and guidance for our spiritual journey.

This woman who chose to live in poverty and humility is greatly admired because she was fueled by a genuine faith and trust in God and a true respect for humanity. She was the Gospel message in action. In the eyes of millions who shared her faith and others who did not, she was a living saint because she touched and transformed them by her boundless love. "There is only one love and this is the love of God," she taught us.

Once we love God deeply enough we will love our neighbor to the same extent because, as we grow in our love for God, we grow to respect all that He has created and to recognize and appreciate all the gifts He has given us. Then naturally we want to take care of all of them. (Mother Teresa, *A Simple Path*, p. 80)

Mother Teresa's mission carries on in her order. The Missionaries of Charity continues to hold the beacon of peace God promised humankind. And it continues its works of love, for, as Mother Teresa said, "our works of love are nothing but the works of peace" (Mother Teresa, *Life in the Spirit*, p. 85).

Mother Teresa left a legacy of loving-kindness and goodness that the world will never forget. She sang her love song loudly to her God.

✧   **Meditation 1**   ✧

# Life in Christ

**Theme**: "It is no longer I who live, but it is Christ who lives in me" (Galatians 2:20).

**Opening prayer:** Dear Lord, grant me the grace, day by day, to be free from whatever prevents me from seeing you in my life, and to realize that my life is real only when it is with you, in you, and for you. Help me to live out your truth and your way and your life, so that I may find my true identity and reach out to others in your name. Amen.

## About Mother Teresa

The work of Mother Teresa and her Missionaries of Charity, even though devoted completely to the poor, did not center around the poor, as has often been represented in the press and as many of us have believed. The truth is that it centered around Jesus Christ. Mother Teresa heard Jesus Christ's voice in the depths of her soul. He called her to serve him by ministering to the poor, and she answered the call. She was anchored in Christ, the center of her life, as she explains here:

> Who is Jesus to me?
> Jesus is the Word made flesh.
> Jesus is the Bread of Life.

Jesus is the Victim offered for our sins on the cross.
Jesus is the sacrifice offered at holy Mass for the sins of
the world and for mine.
Jesus is the word—to be spoken.
Jesus is the truth—to be told.
Jesus is the way—to be walked.
Jesus is the light—to be lit.
Jesus is the life—to be lived.
Jesus is the love—to be loved.
Jesus is the joy—to be shared.
Jesus is the sacrifice—to be offered.
Jesus is the peace—to be given.
Jesus is the Bread of Life—to be eaten.
Jesus is the hungry—to be fed.
Jesus is the thirsty—to be satiated.
Jesus is the naked—to be clothed.
Jesus is the homeless—to be taken in.
Jesus is the sick—to be healed.
Jesus is the lonely—to be loved.
Jesus is the unwanted—to be wanted.
Jesus is the leper—to wash his wounds.
Jesus is the beggar—to give him a smile.
Jesus is the drunkard—to listen to him.
Jesus is the mentally ill—to protect him.
Jesus is the little one—to embrace him.
Jesus is the blind—to lead him.
Jesus is the dumb—to speak for him.
Jesus is the crippled—to walk with him.
Jesus is the drug addict—to befriend him.
Jesus is the prostitute—to remove from danger and
befriend her.
Jesus is the prisoner—to be visited.
Jesus is the old—to be served.

(Pp. 128–129)

To me—
Jesus is my God.
Jesus is my spouse.
Jesus is my life.
Jesus is my only love.

Jesus is my all in all.
Jesus is my everything.
Jesus, I love with my whole heart, with my whole
being.
I have given him all, even my sins, and he has
espoused me to himself in all tenderness and
love.
Now and for life I am the spouse of my crucified
Spouse.

(Mother Teresa, *Jesus*, p. 129)

**Pause:** Think about the way you live your own life. Does Jesus Christ make any difference in your life? Why or why not?

## Mother Teresa's Words

We are contemplatives in the midst of the world because we touch Christ twenty-four hours a day. (Mother Teresa, *Heart of Joy*, p. 53)

Keep the light of Christ always burning in your heart—for he alone is the Way to walk. He is the Life to live. He is the Love to love. (Mother Teresa, *Life in the Spirit*, p. 87)

## Reflection

The secretary general of the United Nations called Mother Teresa the most powerful woman in the world. Indeed, she was—because her only focus and life and love was Jesus Christ. Without him, she could not do anything, but with him, by him, and in him, she was able to move mountains. The power of her prayer, her total acceptance of the will of God, her love of all human life, and her ability to see Christ incarnated in every human being allowed her to say genuinely: "He does it, I do not do it. I am more sure of it than of my own life" (Le Joly, *Mother Teresa*, p. 172).

Mother Teresa's tremendous success and her great influence on people cannot be comprehended in mere human terms. The only plausible explanation is that the entire "Mother Teresa phenomenon" is part of the divine plan for the world. Because her vision was to bring the whole world to Christ, whom alone she loved unconditionally and for whom she worked tirelessly, she was a special gift to Christianity and to the world.

Although her life was poor in material goods, it was rich in Christ, the aim of her true love, her alpha and omega, to whom she belonged. "Our vocation," she strongly affirmed, "is to belong to Jesus, to belong with a conviction, not because my vocation is to work with the poor or to be a contemplative, but because I am called to belong to him in the conviction that nothing can separate me from his love" (Mother Teresa, *Jesus*, p. 65).

Living in Christ was indeed the secret to her ability to preach the Gospel without evangelizing in a propagandist sense. She simply lived for and in Christ every moment of every day, in every situation in which she found herself and with every person she met. For her, Jesus was not only a page of history, Jesus was here and now. He was in the Eucharist. He was flesh and blood. He was in each needy, suffering soul she met. He was in every person. He was a continuous incarnation. He gave meaning to her life. "Jesus explains our life" (Mother Teresa, *My Life*, p. 28), she confessed.

Mother Teresa lost herself in order to find herself in Christ. This is not self-annihilation. It is, rather, a profound inner transformation through which one experiences Christ in all things and all things in Christ. Jesus told his friends, "I am in my Father, and you in me, and I in you" (John 14:20). And Saint Paul wrote, "It is no longer I who live, but it is Christ who lives in me" (Galatians 2:20). Such a transformation is not merely mystical, because it inevitably changes a person's outward life and thereby changes the world. Mother Teresa embodied life in Christ and helped us see that it is available to all.

✧ How do you experience God in your life?

✧ What do you feel when you hear Jesus Christ say to you personally, "You are in me, and I in you"?

✧ What does identification with Jesus Christ mean to you? What does identification with others mean to you? How does your identification with others reflect your identification with Jesus Christ?

✧ Does identification with Christ and others seem a direct path to personal growth? Explain.

✧ What action could you take to make identification with others a real step forward in your life in Christ?

✧ In what ways do you live in Christ?

✧ What makes a community truly Christian? What practical steps could you take now to make your community a great source of energy and support in your own life in Christ?

✧ Sit in a comfortable position. Take a deep breath, slowly and consciously. Say the word "Jesus" as you breathe in and out. Repeat it for several minutes.

## God's Word

Abide in me as I abide in you. Just as the branch cannot bear fruit by itself unless it abides in the vine, neither can you unless you abide in me. I am the vine, you are the branches. Those who abide in me and I in them bear much fruit, because apart from me you can do nothing. Whoever does not abide in me is thrown away like a branch and withers; such branches are gathered, thrown into the fire, and burned. If you abide in me, and my words abide in you, ask for whatever you wish, and it will be done for you. (John 15:4–7)

**Closing prayer:** If, in you, who are the source of my strength, I can do all things (see Philippians 4:13), please, Lord, enable me to yield myself to your love so that you become my very life. Only then can I realize that your infinity is the limitless horizon of my love for you in whomever you choose to dwell.

# ✧ Meditation 2 ✧

# The Urgency of Prayer

**Theme:** "Prayer," said Mother Teresa, "is as necessary as the air, as the blood in our body, as anything to keep us alive—to keep us alive to the grace of God" (Neff, p. 20).

**Opening prayer:** Lord, you said that without you I can do nothing (John 15:5), and your apostle suggested that with you I can do all things (Philippians 4:13). I urge you, dear Lord, to come and dwell in my heart so that I can, through your infinite and unconditional love, live up to all the potential you seeded in me, by doing your will and loving all my sisters and brothers.

## About Mother Teresa

Beirut, Lebanon, has been torn by civil conflict since the mid-1970s. During a visit to that city, Mother Teresa announced that the next day she would cross the fighting lines and reach out to a group of orphaned and crippled children on the other side. Some concerned individuals told her not to go because she would be shot.

She said, "Tomorrow there will be a truce—the fighting will stop." "How do you know, Mother?" they asked her. She replied: "The Sisters have prayed. There will be a cease-fire and truce tomorrow. The Sisters have prayed for it" (Le Joly, *Mother Teresa*, p. 119).

The cease-fire happened. And Mother Teresa went to the other side and took care of the children who desperately needed her protection—God's protection.

Mother Teresa took advantage of every opportunity to share a prayer and to teach prayer. After she won the Nobel Peace Prize, she saw the president of India at a public reception in Delhi. "When he met me," she later recalled, "he pulled out of his coat pocket a card on which I had written the prayer of Newman, 'Jesus shine through me,' which we [the Missionaries of Charity] say daily. I had previously given it to him. The president took out the card from his pocket and told me, 'I say the prayer and it gives me consolation in times of stress and difficulty.'" She added, "I had changed Jesus into Lord, because [the president] is not a Christian" (Le Joly, *Mother Teresa of Calcutta*, p. 215).

All her visitors joined in prayer with her. For her, to pray with them was the apex of the meeting.

**Pause**: Do you feel the urgency of prayer in your life? Do you feel more comfortable and inspired when you pray privately or when you pray with others?

## Mother Teresa's Words

It is not possible to engage in the direct apostolate without being a soul at prayer. . . .

Love to pray—feel the need to pray often during the day and take the trouble to pray. If you want to pray better, you must pray more. Prayer enlarges the heart until it is capable of containing God's gift of himself. Ask and seek and your heart will grow big enough to receive him and keep him as your own. . . .

Prayer to be fruitful must come from the heart and must be able to touch the heart of God. See how Jesus taught his disciples to pray. Call God your Father, praise and glorify his name. Do his will, ask for daily bread, spiritual and temporal, ask for forgiveness of your own sins and that we may forgive others—and also for the grace to be delivered from evil which is in us and around us. (Mother Teresa, *Life in the Spirit,* pp. 17–18)

My secret is quite simple. I pray and through my prayer I become one in love with Christ, and see that praying to him is to love him, and that means to fulfill his words. (Mother Teresa, *Life in the Spirit,* p. 1)

# Reflection

Mother Teresa and her sisters lived their faith. When prayer is directed for the good of souls, it is answered. That is why prayer, not work, always came first in her life.

Mother Teresa shared her convictions about prayer with everyone. She even recommended them to politicians and world leaders.

This international figure was very much "involved" in politics. She advocated justice and compassion for all people, especially the marginalized ones. She spoke to the strongest on behalf of the poorest of the poor. When once asked to give advice to professional politicians, she encouraged them to spend more time in prayer.

Changing systems and laws directly did not interest Mother Teresa; changing people's hearts did. She knew that unjust systems and laws would be addressed by people with changed hearts. As the old adage says, Prayer does not change things; prayer changes people, and people change things. That is why her first prescription for peace and justice was prayer, and why she insisted on prayer. Prayer is powerful.

Mother Teresa knew how to get the things that were needed for her work, and she also knew how to get things done. She trusted her Lord. She counted on the power of the Almighty. Her strategy was this: she prayed, and she asked her sisters also to pray. But her idea of praying was more than just saying words; to her, praying was a relationship of love.

Indeed, prayer should lead us into a deeper encounter with the living God. Though people taken up by an unmerciful activism may see time spent in prayer as a foolish waste, lovers of God cherish it. To them, every minute with God is a treasured gift. Prayer is a love relationship. Prayer brings us closer and closer to God.

This closeness to God is not only possible, it is God's desire for us. God wants us as we are—with our temperaments, our human strengths and weaknesses, our dreams, our failures, our backgrounds, our scars, and our joys. God wants a full relationship with us. We can welcome this relationship with God when we really pray. Our prayer should be the very expression of our deepest love for God and for others. If it is, we will find time for prayer, because we will enjoy immensely our minutes, hours, and days with God, just as we enjoy our time with people we love.

Prayer is relevant, not as a means to change a situation or even the world—although it does that too—but as a love relationship with God and a concerned search for God's designs for us in the world.

Prayer is God's presence to us and our sense of being in that presence. It is communion in God, with God, and with others here on earth. It allows God to reach us in ordinary ways, so that we naturally start to "inhale" God's blessings, and "exhale" praise and thanks. Prayer is thus the "breath of the spirit" and of our true life. Mother Teresa was a living example of it.

✧ Start or add to a prayer diary. Try to include different types of prayer such as praise, worship, petition, thanksgiving, and meditation. Be specific when you pray for someone or something.

✧ Prayer is your communication with God. In communication, there is always an interchange. You speak and you listen, as does God. When you pray, do you really communicate with God? Do you tell God what is in your mind? Do you listen to God—just listen? Are you present to God's communication in every event of your life?

✧ Does God hear all prayers? Does God hear your prayers? Does God hear the prayers of those who do not believe as you believe?

✧ When do you usually call on God? What determines when, where, and how often you pray?

✧ Which of your prayer activities do you find most satisfying? What makes them more satisfying than the others?

✧ What is prayer to you?

✧ Saint Paul advises, "Pray without ceasing" (1 Thessalonians 5:17), and Mother Teresa said, "Prayer for me means becoming twenty-four hours a day at one with the will of Jesus to live for him, through him and with him" (Mother Teresa, *Life in the Spirit*, p. 1). Can you transform your entire life into a prayerful life? That is what you are called to do as a follower of Christ.

## God's Word

Whatever you ask for in prayer with faith, you will receive. (Matthew 21:22)

Whenever you pray, do not be like the hypocrites; for they love to stand and pray in the synagogues and at the street corners, so that they may be seen by others. Truly I tell you, they have received their reward. But whenever you pray, go into your room and shut the door and pray to your Father who is in secret; and your Father who sees in secret will reward you.

When you are praying, do not heap up empty phrases as the Gentiles do; for they think that they will be heard because of their many words. Do not be like them, for your Father knows what you need before you ask him.

Pray then this way:

Our Father in heaven,
    hallowed be your name.
    Your kingdom come.
    Your will be done,
        on earth as it is in heaven.

Give us this day our daily bread.
And forgive us our debts,
>as we also have forgiven our debtors.
And do not bring us to the time of trial,
>but rescue us from the evil one.

>>>>>>(Matthew 6:5–13)

**Closing prayer:** Lord, teach me to pray so that I may grow closer to you and my life will be transformed in you. You are my joy, my hope, my teacher, my friend, my brother, my savior, my redeemer, my heart's desire, my surest guide on this path of life, my very life. I love you, Lord.

✧  **Meditation 3**  ✧

# Silence

**Theme:** "Silence gives us a new outlook on everything," said Mother Teresa. "Listen in silence, because if your heart is full of other things you cannot hear the voice of God" (Neff, p. 22).

**Opening prayer:** In our culture of noise, sound, traffic, and a cacophony of voices advocating different values and policies, and in the midst of the bombardment of high-tech information, allow me, dear Lord, to discern and recognize your voice. Teach me to silence all that is not coming from you. Teach me to listen to your word. Teach me to be silent.

## About Mother Teresa

Mother Teresa told this little story:

> There is a very important theologian, a very holy priest, who is also one of the best in India right now. I know him very well, and I said to him, "Father, you talk all day about God. How close you must be to God! You are talking all the time about God." And you know what he said to me? He said, "I may be talking much about God, but I may be talking very little to God." And then he explained, "I may be rattling off so many words and may be saying many good things, but deep down I have not got

41

the time to listen. Because in the silence of the heart, God speaks." (Neff, p. 21)

According to Mother Teresa, "God is the friend of silence" (Mother Teresa, *Life in the Spirit*, p. 19), and the important thing in our life is not what we say to God but what God says to us. We should be silent in order to listen.

**Pause:** Make yourself a cup of tea and savor it slowly in complete silence.

## Mother Teresa's Words

To make possible true interior silence, we shall practice:
—*Silence of the eyes*, by seeking always the beauty and goodness of God everywhere, closing them to the faults of others and to all that is sinful and disturbing to the soul;
—*Silence of the ears*, by listening always to the voice of God and to the cry of the poor and the needy, closing them to all other voices that come from the evil one or from fallen human nature: e.g., gossip, tale-bearing, and uncharitable words;
—*Silence of the tongue*, by praising God and speaking the life-giving Word of God that is the Truth that enlightens and inspires, brings peace, hope, and joy, and by refraining from self-defense and every word that causes darkness, turmoil, pain, and death;
—*Silence of the mind*, by opening it to the truth and knowledge of God in prayer and contemplation, like Mary who pondered the marvels of the Lord in her heart, and by closing it to all untruths, distractions, destructive thoughts, rash judgment, false suspicions of others, revengeful thoughts, and desires;
—*Silence of the heart*, by loving God with our whole heart, soul, mind, and strength and one another as God loves, desiring God alone and avoiding all selfishness, hatred, envy, jealousy, and greed.

(Neff, pp. 24–25)

# Reflection

Mother Teresa stated, "Man needs silence." In explaining that spiritual principle, she added:

> Once I was asked by someone what I consider most important in the training of the sisters. I answered:
>
> Silence. Interior and exterior silence. Silence is essential in a religious house. The silence of humility, of charity, the silence of the eyes, of the ears, of the tongue. There is no life of prayer without silence.
>
> Silence, and then kindness, charity; silence leads to charity, charity to humility. (Mother Teresa, *My Life*, p. 108)

The schedule of the Missionaries of Charity sets aside a good part of every day and part of every week for silence. At 4:30 in the morning, the sisters start with prayer and meditation, Mass, and Communion. At 2:00 p.m., they have spiritual reading. Six thirty in the evening is reserved for adoration of the Blessed Sacrament. At 9:00 p.m., the members of the order go for night prayers and prepare the meditation of the next morning. And one day every week, they conduct a recollection.

"There is no life of prayer without silence." Mother Teresa was able to silence every possible exterior and interior interference, and let God be God in her and through her to others. She believed that she was an instrument of God—"a pencil" in God's hands (González-Balado, p. 23). And she sought God's will in prayerful silence.

To help foster exterior silence, we must, said Mother Teresa, do these things:

—respect certain times and places of more strict silence;
—move about and work prayerfully, quietly, and gently;
—avoid at all costs all unnecessary speaking and notice;
—speak, when we have to, softly, gently, saying just what is necessary;
—look forward to profound silence as a holy and precious time, a withdrawal into the living silence of God.

(Neff, p. 25)

Interior silence is more difficult to achieve than is exterior silence. But we must make every effort to find it. In the silence of the mind, we will be open to the truth and knowledge of God, and in the silence of the heart, God speaks to us and we listen to God.

Mother Teresa believed that

> if we really want to pray we must first learn to listen, for in the silence of the heart God speaks. And to be able to hear that silence, to be able to hear God we need a clean heart; for a clean heart can see God, can hear God, can listen to God; and then only from the fullness of our heart can we speak to God. But we cannot speak unless we have listened, unless we have made that connection with God in the silence of our heart. (Egan, *Such a Vision*, p. 427)

Only when we learn to listen will we understand that "the essential thing is not what we say but what God says to us and through us" (Neff, p. 22).

Even though Christian life is certainly words and actions, and we have all kinds of reasons to insist on that, it is also listening and just being. It is silence. The Holy Spirit, without outcry and uproar, works in the depths. God speaks to us in silence.

God is present in the fullness of all silence. Silence can be the most eloquent speech.

That is what makes silence unique in our life, especially when it is not only a silence of the tongue but also a silence of our uncontrolled imagination, inordinate desires, paralyzing fears, and other disturbing agitations and barriers that stand between us and God. In silence, we convey God's message, not ours.

Real silence allows God to speak through us without interference from us or from outside forces. Real silence is a declaration of being in love with God and with all the faces of God. Real silence lets God be the all in all. Mother Teresa lived an eloquent silence.

✧ Do you feel the need to leave the radio or television on all the time? Does silence scare you? Does noise, any noise, bother you, or does it rather reassure you? Try to experience two minutes of complete silence, then share what you feel.

✧ Do you sometimes project a talkative, busy, on-the-go personality to others? If so, is that your true self? Who are you deep inside, in the silent spaces of your being?

✧ Do you feel sometimes a need to get away from the noise and tension of modern life in order to relax and find a sense of inner unity, reconciliation, and integration? Consider going to a silent retreat.

✧ When we live outside ourselves, we are divided and pulled in many directions. Silence helps us to draw in our dissipated energies and concentrate on the purpose of our life. Have you ever contemplated to define your own mission in life, your priorities, and your purposes?

✧ Use the extract under "Mother Teresa's Words" as a guided meditation, pausing after each item in the list and pondering its meaning for you.

✧ Mother Teresa said: "See how nature, the trees, the flowers, and the grass grow in perfect silence. See the stars, the moon, and the sun, how they move in silence" (Neff, p. 26). Go outside and participate in their silence. Ponder how you can glorify God by just being what you really are.

✧ Shut out every noise around you for a few minutes. Be silent. Close your eyes gently. Take a deep breath. Invite God to your inner self. Listen. Just listen. After a moment or two, share what you have experienced. Did you hear God's message to you?

## God's Word

Be still, and know that I am God! (Psalm 46:10)

Immediately [Jesus] made the disciples get into the boat and go on ahead to the other side, while he dismissed the crowds. And after he had dismissed the crowds, he went up the mountain by himself to pray. When evening came, he was there alone. (Matthew 14:22–23)

[Jesus] withdrew from [the disciples] about a stone's throw, knelt down, and prayed. (Luke 22:41)

He would withdraw to deserted places and pray. (Luke 5:16)

**Closing prayer:** Dear God, my ears, eyes, mind, and heart are cluttered with so many noises, so many mirages, so many clingings, that I can hardly grasp your voice, see your light, and follow your way. Dear God, grant me, with my daily bread, my daily silence. Amen.

# ✧ Meditation 4 ✧

# Love at the Center

**Theme**: "We have been created in order to love and to be loved" (Mother Teresa, *Jesus*, p. 57), said Mother Teresa. Love must be at the center of everyone's life. Life is for loving.

**Opening prayer:** God, help us to love one another as you love us. Inspire us to reach out to one another in compassion and to give freely of ourselves and our love. Amen.

## About Mother Teresa

To illustrate how God's love works, Mother Teresa liked to tell the following story:

> A man came to our house and said, "My only child is dying! The doctor has prescribed a medicine that you can get only in England." (Now I have permission from our government to store life-saving medicines that are gathered from all over the country. We have many people that go from house to house and gather leftover medicines. And they bring them to us and we give them to our poor people. We have thousands of people who come to our dispensaries.) While we were talking, a man came in with a basket of medicines.

I looked at that basket of medicines: right on the top was the very medicine that man needed for his dying child! If it had been underneath, I wouldn't have seen it.

If he had come earlier or later, I would not have remembered. He came just in time.

I stood in front of that basket and I was thinking, "There are millions of children in the world, and God is concerned with that little child in the slums of Calcutta. To send that man at that very moment! To put the medicine right on the top, so I could see it!"

See God's tender concern for you and for me! He would do the same thing for each one of you. (Neff, p. 258)

Mother Teresa demonstrated her own love for the poor when Pope Paul VI took part in the Thirty-eighth International Eucharistic Congress, in 1964, in Bombay. During that visit, the pope used a white Lincoln given to him by a group of Catholics from the United States. Before he was ready to board the plane back to Rome, the pope announced that he would leave the car to Mother Teresa, to use in her mission of love. Mother Teresa was moved by the pope's gesture and thanked him gratefully. But she never set foot in that car. Instead, she raffled it off, and with the proceeds she built a center for the rehabilitation of people with leprosy.

**Pause**: Think of a time you were able to help someone who was in difficulty, just out of love.

## Mother Teresa's Words

You may be exhausted with work, even kill yourself, but unless your work is interwoven with love it is useless. (Mother Teresa, *Jesus*, p. 21)

Love is a fruit in season at all times. (Mother Teresa, *Heart of Joy*, p. 68)

Do not pursue spectacular deeds. What matters is the gift of your self, the degree of love that you put into each one of your actions. (Mother Teresa, *Heart of Joy*, p. 61)

We can do no great things—only small things with great love. (Mother Teresa, *Life in the Spirit*, p. 45)

Where God is, there is love. (Mother Teresa, *My Life*, p. 75)

If we pray
    we will believe
If we believe
    we will love
If we love
    we will serve.

Only then can we put
    our love for God
    into living action
Through service of Christ
    in the distressing
    disguise of the Poor.

           (Mother Teresa, *Life in the Spirit*, p. 1)

It is easy to love those who live far away. It is not always easy to love those who live right next to us. It is easier to offer a dish of rice to meet the hunger of a needy person than to comfort the loneliness and the anguish of someone in our own home who does not feel loved. (Mother Teresa, *Heart of Joy*, p. 120)

## Reflection

Before her name was on the lips of millions and millions of people around the world, Mother Teresa was quietly living her love story with her Lord, Jesus Christ, who was "in the distressing disguise" of the abandoned, the neglected, the destitute, and the dying—all of those who became familiar with her gentle voice and her warm dedication. In every speech she made and in every action she performed, she always mentioned her relationship with the loving God.

Mother Teresa accepted material help for the poor. But she did not ask for it. Instead, she insisted that the needy, especially those who are children, require love, affection, and companionship before bread, milk, vitamins, and toys. She wanted people to offer the most precious gift of all—themselves—and to do so in and through love. When invited to address the National Council of Catholic Women of the United States, she surprised everyone by saying:

> I don't come to ask for anything. I have never done that since we began this work. When I meet with a group of people . . . as I am now meeting here with you, I simply tell them: "I have come to offer you the opportunity to do something beautiful for God." And the people give evidence of wanting to do something beautiful for God. And they step forward. (González-Balado, p. 9)

She inspired people, awakened their minds, and motivated a compassionate love in their hearts.

Mother Teresa was never convinced of the popular notion that the bigger the donation is, the more it is worth. For her, the value of giving was determined by the intensity of love, not the size of the gift. She was profoundly grateful when a beggar wanted to give her all that he had collected in one day. His was a very little gift indeed. But in her eyes, it was everything. The beggar's gesture touched her somehow more deeply than even the Nobel Prize for peace. Like the widow in the Gospel who offered what she had to live on, just "two small copper coins" (Luke 21:2), this beggar was considered more generous than the rich who offer from their surplus.

Mother Teresa always recommended: "Give until it hurts, because real love hurts. That is why you must love until it hurts" (Mother Teresa, *One Heart*, p. 8). Loving until it hurts is the key to the paradoxical relationship that is established between those who have and those who have not. And it could be an effective strategy for both the rich and the poor. Love is never wrong. Love is for living. Love is the most important element for healing others, the earth, and ourselves.

✧ Mother Teresa said: "We must love one another as God loved us who gave us his only Son. We must love without limit as Jesus did who died out of love for us" (Le Joly, *Mother Teresa*, p. 80). Why, do you think, is love so important? Is it because Christianity is about reaching the fullness of life by entering deeply into the lives of others?

✧ What inspires you to love others? Is it your experience of being loved? Is it your awareness of Jesus Christ as a guide, a model, and a friend? Is it the recommendation of the Bible and all saints? Is it the example of a loving person? Describe your inspiration in your journal, perhaps using a poem or story format.

✧ What do you think true love is—an emotion? A concern? A caring action? An understanding? Or what?

✧ Read 1 Corinthians 13:1–13. Does Saint Paul help your understanding of love?

✧ Do you know God? If so, does your knowledge of God come through your parents, your church, the Bible, books, or what? Have you ever known God through experiencing God's love?

✧ Share some of the commitments to which you have been faithful. Describe some of your actions that carry God's love to others.

✧ What do you appreciate more, the gift or the love behind the gift?

✧ Write a three-line prayer of gratitude for the gift of love.

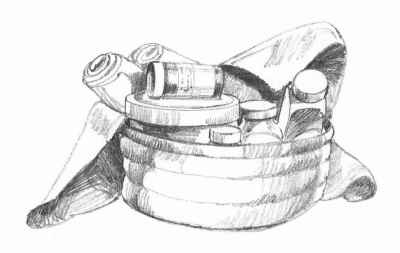

## God's Word

This is my commandment, that you love one another as I have loved you. (John 15:12)

God is love, and those who abide in love abide in God, and God abides in them. (1 John 4:16)

Those who say, "I love God," and hate their brothers or sisters, are liars. (1 John 4:20)

**Closing prayer:** Loving God, I want your love to be the very center of my life. Please help me to live fully in your love and to live your love as fully as I can, here and now. For I understand that the only question you will ask me the day you call me home is, "How much have you loved?"

✧   **Meditation 5**   ✧

# Minding the Call

**Theme:** Our inner call makes us fully alive, stirs up joy in our heart, motivates us, frees us, and gives meaning to our life.

**Opening prayer:** God, open my mind and heart to listen to your voice, discern your plan for my life, and follow your call wherever it might lead me.

## About Mother Teresa

At an early age, Mother Teresa was convinced that God was calling her to be a nun. She was happy about that, especially when her mother, who had opposed her at first, told her: "All right, my daughter, you go. But be careful to be always of God and Christ, only." "Not only God," said Mother Teresa, "but also [my mother] would have condemned me if I had not followed my vocation with faithfulness. She will ask me one day, 'My daughter, have you lived only for God?'" (Mother Teresa, *My Life*, p. 1). However, to be sure that she was heading down the right path, Mother Teresa sought advice from her confessor. She asked him, "How can I know if God is calling me and for what he is calling me?" He responded: "You will know by your happiness. If you are happy with the idea that God calls you to serve him and your neighbor, this will be the proof of your vocation. Profound joy of the heart is like a magnet that indicates the path of life. One has to follow it, even though one enters into a way full of difficulties" (p. 2).

Mother Teresa became the happiest nun. But that was not enough for her:

> It was on the tenth of September 1946, in the train that took me to Darjeeling, the hill station in the Himalayas, that I heard the call of God.
>
> In quiet, intimate prayer with our Lord, I heard distinctly, a call within a call.
>
> The message was quite clear: I was to leave the convent and help the poor whilst living among them. It was an order. I knew where I belonged, but I did not know how to get there.
>
> I felt intensely that Jesus wanted me to serve him among the poorest of the poor, the uncared for, the slum dwellers, the abandoned, the homeless. Jesus invited me to serve him and follow him in actual poverty, to practice a kind of life that would make me similar to the needy in whom he was present, suffered and loved. (P. 8)

Her inspiration came in a simple, ordinary, slow-moving means of transportation, through a mystical experience that made the event sacred.

Then she had to wait. She had to comply with a rigorous ecclesiastical legislation by asking the pope for special authorization to leave the Sisters of Loreto. She waited even though her call was a passionate call, and maybe because it was passionate; a passionate heart never gives up. It took two years to get that so-waited-for permission. Finally, on 16 August 1948, she was allowed to pursue her new calling, her new call within a call. That day marked the opening of a new chapter that changed her life and had a great impact on the history of Christianity and the world at large.

**Pause:** Have you ever pondered your own call? Is what you are doing now what you are supposed to do? Is what you seem to be now what you are meant to be?

## Mother Teresa's Words

If there are people who feel that God wants them to change the structure of society, that is something between them and their God. We must serve him in whatever way we are called.

I am called to help the individual, to love each poor person, not to deal with institutions. I am in no position to judge. (Mother Teresa, *My Life*, p. 103)

At Loreto I was the happiest nun in the world. Leaving the work I did there was a great sacrifice. What I did not have to leave was being a religious sister.

The Sisters of Loreto were devoted to teaching, which is a genuine apostolate for Christ. But my specific vocation, within the religious vocation, was for the poorest poor. It was a call from inside my vocation—like a second vocation. It was a command to resign Loreto, where I was happy, in order to serve the poor in the streets. (Mother Teresa, *Heart of Joy*, p. 39)

# Reflection

Everyone is unique. Everyone has a special role to play in the world. Everyone has to be themselves. To be who we are is God's call to you and me. Mother Teresa was unique.

Our call is the driving force that frees us. It enables us to be aware of what really matters, to focus our attention and love, to be captivated by something, by a cause, by Someone much greater than ourselves. By answering our call, we lose ourselves in order to find ourselves in the mystery of life. This is why knowing our true selves and being faithful to our special call—the truth of our own life—is essential. Our deepest call is our contribution to the world. Mother Teresa knew her special call. She followed it. She made a difference in the world, a big difference.

Because our individual call is something special, there is no typical call to serve as a model, nor are there strict rules for all calls. A call might come in a train, like Mother Teresa's second call did, or it might come in a moment of truth, in a prayer, in an act of kindness, in the activity of reading a book, or in our sleep. It might also be discovered over a long period of time, through a process that requires step-by-step choices and the help and experiences of others.

Our call might expand over time to include new avenues of service that become open to us as we grow and change. We might receive a new call within our call, as Mother Teresa did. Or we might receive a new call altogether, one that leads us down a different path of love and inspiration.

In the final analysis, a profound longing for God is the basis for all calls. Nevertheless, a personal call will take a tangible form—such as the priesthood, religious life, marriage, missionary work, or service for others—that reflects who we really are. It will not come in a vacuum.

No matter what our call is and how it comes, we are to be faithful to it in our ordinary life on a daily basis.

Our call is the source of our deep joy in life because it is our truth and truth makes us free.

God calls us to be who we are. Who we are is our involvement in and contribution to life and our particular path to God. It is also the way that allows God to work in us and through us. God called Mother Teresa to work with the poorest of the poor.

✧ Choose a quiet place. Be silent. Take a deep breath. Be alone with God and with the desire of following God's will. Say to God, "Speak, for your servant is listening" (1 Samuel 3:10). Describe the movements you experience within you during this time.

✧ What makes you feel alive, enthusiastic, and eager? What makes you feel bored, depressed, and unmotivated—unable to move?

✧ What do you like about yourself? What do you not like?

✧ Name some options you are facing. Consider each one of them in turn. Do you feel enthusiasm or a lack of interest or something else when you think of choosing it?

✧ Think about an option you are choosing right now. Does it make you want to grow? Write a dialogue with Jesus Christ in which you explore the ways it might help you do so.

✧ What is your strongest goal at this time in your life? Where is your main focus? Do you have a vision?

✧ Name some things that prevent you from reaching an inner quiet and an inner freedom.

✧ What is your answer to this question: Who am I?

✧ Repeat several times, "God, I am listening."

# God's Word

I pray that the God of our Lord Jesus Christ, the Father of glory, may give you a spirit of wisdom and revelation as you come to know him, so that, with the eyes of your heart enlightened, you may know what is the hope to which he has called you. (Ephesians 1:17–18)

You did not choose me but I chose you. And I appointed you to go and bear fruit. (John 15:16)

The gifts and the calling of God are irrevocable. (Romans 11:29)

All who exalt themselves will be humbled, and all who humble themselves will be exalted. (Matthew 23:12)

Consider your own call, brothers and sisters: not many of you were wise by human standards, not many were powerful, not many were of noble birth. But God chose what is foolish in the world to shame the wise; God chose what is weak in the world to shame the strong; God chose what is low and despised in the world, things that are not, to reduce to nothing things that are, so that no one might boast in the presence of God. (1 Corinthians 1:26–29)

**Closing prayer:** God, often I am not sure of my special call. But at every time in my life and in all that I do, make your will my will, and your heart my heart.

# A Life for the Poor

**Theme:** God has identified with those who are hungry, thirsty, strangers, naked, sick, homeless, and in prison—the poor.

**Opening prayer:** Lord, open my eyes and my heart to those who are poor. Let me see you in those who are hungry, alone, hurt, and afraid. Show me how to help and serve them in your name.

## About Mother Teresa

The poor, for Mother Teresa, are all those of broken body, mind, heart, and soul. She said, "They may be far or near, materially poor or spiritually poor, hungry for love and friendship, ignorant of the riches of the love of God for them, homeless for want of a home made of love in your heart" (Mother Teresa, *Life in the Spirit*, p. 15).

God is not an abstraction, or a system, or a concept—even the most perfect one. God is tangible reality, working in and through the poor and those who serve them. Mother Teresa explained:

The other day, one of our sisters was washing a leper covered with wounds.

A Muslim priest was standing by and said, "All these years I have believed that Jesus Christ is a prophet. But today I believe Jesus Christ is God if he is able to give such joy to this sister, enabling her to do her work with so much love!" (Mother Teresa, *My Life*, p. 60)

The poor, for Mother Teresa, are great. They are vulnerable as we are. They are transformed by our attention, care, and love, and they transform us in the same process. Mother Teresa explained this too:

> I will never forget something that happened when I was at Loreto. One of the children was very, very naughty. She was only six or seven years old. One day, when she was extremely naughty, I took her hand and said, "Come, we're going for a walk." She had some money with her. One hand held my hand and the other held tightly to the money. "I will buy this, I will buy that," she kept saying. Suddenly she saw a blind beggar, and at once she left the money with him. From that day she was a completely different child. She had been so small and so naughty. Yet that one decision changed her life. It is the same with you. Get rid of anything that's holding you back. If you want to be all for Jesus, the decision has to come from within you. (Neff, pp. 215–216)

**Pause:** What holds you back from helping anyone who needs you?

## Mother Teresa's Words

We need to understand the poor. There is not only material poverty but also spiritual poverty, which is harder and deeper, harboring even in the hearts of very wealthy men. Wealth is not only property and money, but our attachment to these things and our abuse of them.

When things become our masters, we are very poor. And so as long as there are rich people who commit excess and do not use things according to the mind of God, there will be poverty in the world. (Mother Teresa, *Heart of Joy*, p. 123)

The poor are great. We have to love them, but not with pity love. We have to love them because it is Jesus who hides under the likeness of the poor. They are our brothers and sisters. They belong to us. The lepers, the dying, the starving, the naked—all of them are Jesus. (Mother Teresa, *Heart of Joy*, p. 6)

Do we know our poor people? Do we know the poor in our house, in our family? Perhaps they are not hungry for a piece of bread. Perhaps our children, husband, wife, are not hungry, or naked, or dispossessed, but are you sure there is no one there who feels unwanted, deprived of affection? Where is your elderly father or mother? (Neff, p. 220)

## Reflection

To see "Mother Teresa" and "the poor" in the same sentence does not surprise us. In fact, we expect to find Mother Teresa associated with the poor.

Mother Teresa devoted her life to the poor. "I have accepted the responsibility of representing the poor of the world" (Mother Teresa, *My Life*, p. 102), she said. She worked in direct contact with them and showed an unlimited goodness toward them. They were concrete individuals in whom she saw and touched and served Jesus Christ himself.

Poverty, for Mother Teresa, was not an intellectual concept; it was a living experience. She said: "To know the problem of poverty intellectually is not to understand it. It is not by reading, taking a walk in the slums, admiring and regretting that we come to understand it and to discover what it has of bad and good. We have to dive into it, live it, share it" (Mother Teresa, *Life in the Spirit*, pp. 55–56).

For her, the poor were real people. They were the hungry, the thirsty, the homeless, the sick, the handicapped, the aged, the imprisoned, the lonely, the comfortless, the bad-tempered, the outcasts, the outsiders, and the materially and spiritually destitute.

Mother Teresa found herself privileged to serve all of them, because she saw Jesus Christ in every one of them. She did what she did, not from a condescending or pitying attitude but with a sincere, positive, and vibrant love for them— for "the poor are great and lovable people" (Mother Teresa, *Heart of Joy,* p. 106), she said.

One day, Mother Teresa heard about a woman and her children who were so poor that they had gone many days without eating anything. Mother Teresa brought them some rice. Immediately, the woman took half the rice and left. After a short time, she came back. Mother Teresa, surprised, asked her where she had gone and what she had done with the rice. The woman answered that her neighbor and the neighbor's children had gone the same number of days without eating, and she wanted to share the rice with them. "The poor are wonderful people" (p. 125), observed Mother Teresa.

Mother Teresa loved the poor so much that she was criticized for spoiling them, by giving them what they needed at the moment without doing something to ameliorate their condition. Her answer was that she wanted to deal more with the individual, not with the crowd and much less with the system and the concept. She wanted to reach the deepest level of all, the human heart. She believed that when the heart is changed, alterations to systems and political situations will emerge naturally.

In their work with the poor, what made Mother Teresa and her sisters credible, and trusted and effective, was that they chose to be poor themselves. They cared for the poor as equals, as friends, and as people of the same condition, just as Jesus did. "We and our poor will depend entirely on Divine Providence both for our material and spiritual needs" (Neff, p. 214), she said.

Because "there is not only material poverty but also spiritual poverty, which is harder and deeper" (Mother Teresa, *Heart of Joy,* p. 123), Mother Teresa and her sisters offered more than food and shelter and medicines and company. They offered at the same time the Reign of God, where meaning of life is recovered, and where human dignity is recognized and deep joy in and with God is treasured.

Poverty is not necessarily a virtue when it means just the lack of the means to satisfy the basic needs of human life, or the injustice caused by the enrichment of others, or the establishment's victimization of those who happen to be weak. Poverty is also not a virtue when it means a lack of health, education, or connection.

Poverty is a virtue—a fine and desirable virtue—when it becomes an evangelical way of life. That implies a spirit of total availability and trusting surrender to God. It means receiving everything from God, and placing everything in service to meet the needs of others according to the will of God. In this sense, poverty heralds the policy of the Reign of God—the ultimate project of Christian life. The poor then become the synonym of the simple, the detached, the ready to give and receive, the trusting, the loving, and the caring. That is to say, poverty becomes the opposite of arrogance, selfishness, self-promotion, self-centeredness, and the Pharisaism so criticized by Jesus in the Gospel.

To choose to be poor, in this virtuous sense, is revolutionary. For when one does so, one then has the courage to face a culture of the domination of the strongest, the most intelligent, the most powerful, the most selfish, and the most aggressive. And by making a radical conversion of the heart, one challenges all systems, ideologies, patterns of acquisitiveness, superfluity of possessions, and lifestyles that do not put God first. Jesus lived this radical way of life. His followers try to do the same.

The bottom line of all virtues, poverty included, is not being just politically and technically correct. The bottom line is love. Poverty may or may not lead to love. But true love always leads to poverty. For when we love God enough to allow the Word of God to penetrate us and adjust our convictions, principles, systems, and ways of living, and allow God to provide for our needs, we do not need to take anything for the journey (see Mark 6:8).

Truly, love is the only foundation there is. A person in love wants to share food, money, medicines, shelter, caring concerns, and above all, God. Mother Teresa shared it all, including above all the love of God. Her life was well rooted in the Gospel. She strove to address the needs of the poor by fulfilling faithfully these words of Jesus Christ:

> I was hungry and you gave me food, I was thirsty and you gave me something to drink, I was a stranger and you welcomed me, I was naked and you gave me clothing, I was sick and you took care of me, I was in prison and you visited me. . . . Truly I tell you, just as you did it to one of the least of these who are members of my family, you did it to me. (Matthew 25:35–40)

✧ Read Matthew 6:25–34. If poverty means emptying your mind and soul of material concerns in order to fill your heart with the Word of God, what practical steps can you take to do that?

✧ Read Matthew 25:31–36. What does that text tell you personally?

✧ Mother Teresa asked, "Do we know the poor in our house, in our family?" (Neff, p. 220). Do you? If so, how can you help them?

✧ Name three material things to which you are attached. To some extent, do those things possess you and run your life? If so, why?

✧ Do you enjoy financial security? Whether you do or not, what are some ways you can share with others, especially those who are less fortunate?

✧ Take a tour of your house with an observing eye. How many things do you have, in every closet and in every corner, that you do not use and most likely will never use? Does the freedom of simple living appeal to you? How can you simplify your life?

✧ Take the same tour within your being. How many concepts, desires, plans, false judgments, prejudices, old resentments, and so on, are sitting there cluttering your mind and crippling your life? When can you start to rely on God alone and to feel free at last?

# God's Word

Give to everyone who begs from you, and do not refuse anyone who wants to borrow from you. (Matthew 5:42)

Whoever has two coats must share with anyone who has none; and whoever has food must do likewise. (Luke 3:11)

If a brother or sister is naked and lacks daily food, and one of you says to them, "Go in peace; keep warm and eat your fill," and yet you do not supply their bodily needs, what is the good of that? (James 2:15–16)

He ordered them to take nothing for their journey except a staff; no bread, no bag, no money in their belts; but to wear sandals and not to put on two tunics. (Mark 6:8–9)

Blessed are the poor in spirit, for theirs is the kingdom of heaven. (Matthew 5:3)

**Closing prayer:** Dearest Lord, grant that I will see you in every one of my brothers and sisters I meet today. I know you can be hiding behind the unattractive disguise of my poor neighbor, my irritable coworker, my unreasonable boss, and the many lonely people of my community. Do not allow me to disgrace your loving gift to me by giving way to impatience with any one of them, or to coldness, unkindness, or indifference. Make me do for others what I do for you.

✧   **Meditation 7**   ✧

# Contemplation in the Heart of the World

**Theme:** Mother Teresa was convinced that "active and contemplative are not two different lives; it is only that one is faith in action through service, the other faith in action through prayer" (Mother Teresa, *Jesus*, p. 66).

**Opening prayer:** In silence and contemplation, I search for you, Lord. In word and deed, I do your will. Guide my search and my actions, that both may be driven by your love and that both may bring your love to others.

## About Mother Teresa

Mother Teresa said:

> One of our brothers came to me in distress . . . and said to me, "My vocation is to work for the lepers. . . . I want to spend my whole life, my everything in this vocation." Then I said to him, "You are making a mistake, Brother; your vocation is to belong to Jesus. He has chosen you for himself, and the work you do is only a means to express your love for him in action. Therefore it does not matter what work you are doing; the main thing is that you belong to him, that you are his, and that he gives you the

means to do this for him." . . . For all of us religious, it does not matter what we do or where we are, as long as we remember that we belong to him, that we are his, that he can do with us what he wants. (Le Joly, *Mother Teresa of Calcutta*, p. 162)

For Mother Teresa, our belonging first to Christ points to the importance of contemplation in her life and in her teachings. But she never saw a separation between contemplation and action. In her meeting with the brother who worked with lepers, she did not deny his vocation, but reminded him that first and foremost he was called to Jesus Christ, and that whatever he did or was had to be through Jesus Christ. To support her conviction, she often used Saint Thomas Aquinas's words:

St. Thomas Aquinas says, "Those who have been called to action would be wrong to think that they are dispensed of contemplative life. Both tasks go closely together. Thus, these two lives, far from being mutually exclusive, involve one another, carrying with them the same means and helps and being mutually complemented. If action is to be fruitful, it needs contemplative life. And the latter, when it reaches a given degree of intensity, spreads part of its surplus over the first." (Neff, pp. 27–28)

**Pause:** Do you separate your daily (active) life from your Christian (contemplative) life?

## Mother Teresa's Words

My sisters and brothers, the Missionaries of Charity, are not social workers: they are contemplatives in the midst of the world. Their lives are consecrated to the Eucharist through contact with Christ under the appearance of bread and under the sorrowful countenance of the poor. (Mother Teresa, *Heart of Joy*, p. 2)

We are called to be contemplatives in the heart of the world by—

—seeking the face of God in everything, everyone, everywhere, all the time, and his hand in every happening;
—seeing and adoring the presence of Jesus, especially in
the lowly appearance of bread, and in the distressing
disguise of the poor, by praying the work, that is, by doing it with Jesus, for Jesus, and to Jesus.

(Neff, p. 28)

# Reflection

Mother Teresa went straight to the point in the speeches
she made, and in her silence when she just lived her life. Because she knew her Gospel and the position of her church, she
seemed to have always clear in her mind the answer she wanted to give. She was not interested in argument and speculation. She was not interested in dividing and analyzing. She
did not see a separation between sacred and profane, between
the spiritual realm and the world, between what she said and
what she did, or between Jesus Christ and others. She lived
Jesus Christ's life. And living Jesus Christ's life was, in essence, living contemplatively. She said: "To me, contemplation
is not to be shut up in a dark place, but to allow Jesus to live
his Passion, his love, his humility in us, praying with us, being
with us, sanctifying through us" (Mother Teresa, *Jesus*, p. 73).

This is why she was able to be, with her sisters and brothers, contemplative in the heart of the world without necessarily withdrawing to desert places. She was also clear about her
functions. She repeatedly stated that she was not a social
worker, even if she did the same work as a social worker. She
was a contemplative, because Jesus Christ was always her focus: "We [the Missionaries of Charity] are with Jesus twenty-
four hours a day. We do everything for Jesus. We do it to
Jesus" (Mother Teresa, *My Life*, p. 61).

Being with Jesus Christ twenty-four hours a day means
being with him in the fullness of life. "Our contemplation is
our life," she explained. "It is not a matter of doing but being.
It is the possession of our spirit by the Holy Spirit breathing
into us the plenitude of God and sending us forth to the whole
creation as his personal message of love" (Neff, pp. 26–27), for

we are meant to be "carriers of God's love" (Mother Teresa, *My Life*, p. 14).

If our love for God involves reaching out to others, contemplation must fruit in action. In other words, this world is God's, and salvation is God's plan for it. God is at work in the world through us. Mother Teresa explained: "He does it, I do not do it" (Le Joly, *Mother Teresa*, p. 172).

Contemplation is about growth in love. It is about being in love continuously, in communion and harmony with the All in all.

In the past, contemplative life was, in a sense, more formal and more rigid. A contemplative dropped all worldly things in order to focus on, in Jesus' words, "the better part" (see Luke 10:38–42). That certainly is a valid interpretation of a life of contemplation, but it is not the only one.

The other approach to a contemplative life, especially in modern times, is to consider the "better part" not as that which is left over after dropping all other things, but as that which includes all else. This is a fine and subtle point. Contemplation is not a separate entity apart from what we do. Instead, contemplation is in the action, in the very process.

According to Mother Teresa, we are to savor God's fullness and faithfulness in the very doing, because God is with us twenty-four hours a day. This is called living by the Word, with the Word, and for the Word. When we do this, our very action becomes contemplation, not because action is necessary for God, but because God's presence in action makes action necessary. Mother Teresa insisted on seeing Jesus Christ in the poorest of the poor because she was driven by the belief that what she was doing for the poor was done for Jesus Christ himself.

A contemplative does not do this or that job to score points for a contemplative life. A contemplative is a person of God, whose business is God's life, the one necessary thing that includes all the other things to be sanctified. Such a person lives in the transforming presence of God in all things, where the dichotomy between the sacred and the secular vanishes as does the separation between action and prayer. When we live in this Presence, said Mother Teresa, we "pray the work, to make the work our love for God in action" (Mother Teresa,

*Jesus*, p. 59), and we find the divine presence everywhere in the unity of all things.

In Christian life, our love for God and for our sisters and brothers is one and the same. We give to others what we have contemplated. We love this tree, this thing, this person, and God at the same time. Being in love with the All in all is the very essence of contemplation.

✧ You know that God understands you, loves you, and knows what you experience every day—your journey, your struggles, your rest, your work—all your ways. How do you react to that knowledge? Do you feel loved? Supported? Fearful? Unworthy? Joyful? Indifferent? Burdened? Strengthened?

✧ God is present in your healthy self and in your light side, as well as in your brokenness, vulnerability, confusion, and dark side. How do you describe God's presence in your inner darkness and vulnerability? Is it quiet? Threatening? Vengeful? Compassionate? Sad? Loving? Transforming?

✧ Do you allow God to run your life with you? Do you surrender to God's will? Do you look at doing what you are supposed to do according to God's design for your life?

✧ What is your reaction to the idea of God's shaping of you? Do you feel loved? Grateful? Angry? Wondering? Rebellious? In your journal, write a dialogue in which you share that reaction with God.

✧ Jesus led an active life, and yet he was contemplative. What can you do to live, as Jesus lived, an active yet contemplative life? Can Mother Teresa help you find a way to do that?

✧ Read Luke 10:38–42. Suppose that Jesus were coming to your home today. How would you welcome him?

✧ Thomas Merton said that contemplation is the perfection of love. Others describe contemplation as the art of paying a loving attention to God in the depth of our being and in

God's world. If love is at the heart of contemplation, what steps can you take to grow in love with God?

✧ "Be still, and know that I am God!" (Psalm 46:10). Be still in God's presence. Repeat the word "God" while looking at a candle or a crucifix. Center yourself in the present moment. Listen. What is God revealing to you?

## God's Word

I pray . . . that Christ may dwell in your hearts through faith, as you are being rooted and grounded in love. (Ephesians 3:16–17)

Those who abide in me and I in them bear much fruit. (John 15:5)

O taste and see that the LORD is good;
    happy are those who take refuge in him.

(Psalm 34:8)

Oh, how I love your law!
    It is my meditation all day long.
Your commandment makes me wiser than my enemies,
    for it is always with me.

(Vv. 97–98)

How sweet are your words to my taste,
    sweeter than honey to my mouth!

(V. 103)

Your decrees are my heritage forever;
    they are the joy of my heart.
I incline my heart to perform your statutes
    forever, to the end.

(Psalm 119:111–112)

**Closing prayer:**

Lord Jesus,
    Come now and make your dwelling in me.
    Be with me among my books, my daydreams, and the pots and pans of my kitchen.
    Be with me through the traffic of the road, on the job, and in the several stores I need to visit today.
    Be with me in the meetings I attend, the people I see, and all the discussions that take place.
    For when you are with me, dear Lord, I feel more connected with others, and whatever I do becomes a meditation.
    What really matters, above all, is to be in love with you twenty-four hours a day. Amen.

# The Secret of Joy

**Theme:** Joy and holiness are intimately interrelated. When holiness unfolds in the context of our daily life, joy increases in the same process. Deep joy is growth in holiness.

### Opening prayer:

I smile, and the world smiles with me.
I laugh, and the world laughs too.
I praise you, dear God, and the world breaks out in song.
For you are the source of my joy,
    the wellspring of my love,
    the key to my compassion.
Be with me today, tomorrow, and forever,
    that I may bring your joy to all I meet.

## About Mother Teresa

Eileen Egan writes:

Mother Teresa often gave people unexpected advice. When a group of Americans visited her in Calcutta, they asked her for some advice to take home to their families.
"Smile at your wives," she told them. "Smile at your husbands."

Thinking perhaps that the advice was simplistic, coming from an unmarried person, one of them asked, "Are you married?"

"Yes," she replied to their surprise, "and I find it very hard sometimes to smile at Jesus. He can be very demanding." (At Prayer, p. 126)

Mother Teresa liked to tell the following story:

Some years have gone by but I will never forget a young French girl who came to Calcutta one day.

She looked so worried. She went to work in our home for dying destitutes. Then, after ten days, she came to see me.

She hugged me and said, "I've found Jesus!"

I asked where she found Jesus.

"In the home for dying destitutes," she answered.

"And what did you do after you found him?"

"I went to confession and Holy Communion for the first time in fifteen years."

Then I said again, "What else did you do?"

"I sent my parents a telegram saying that I found Jesus."

I looked at her and I said, "Now, pack up and go home. Go home and give joy, love, and peace to your parents."

She went home radiating joy, because her heart was filled with joy. She went home, and what joy she brought to her family!

Why?

Because she had lost the innocence of her youth and had gotten it back again. (Neff, p. 118)

Mother Teresa was convinced that the Lord was the key secret of joy. When one finds the Lord, one finds joy.

**Pause:** What is a source of joy for you?

## Mother Teresa's Words

Joy is prayer; joy is strength; joy is love, a net of love by which you can catch souls. God loves a cheerful giver. He gives most who gives with joy. If in the work you have difficulties and you accept them with joy, with a big smile—in this, as in any other good thing—they will see your good works and glorify the Father. The best way to show your gratitude to God and people is to accept everything with joy. A joyful heart is the normal result of a heart burning with love. (Mother Teresa, *Jesus*, p. 127)

Cheerfulness is indeed the fruit of the Holy Spirit and a clear sign of the kingdom within. Jesus shared his joy with his disciples: "that my joy may be in you and that your joy be full" (Jn 15:11). Our joy is a work of our generosity, selflessness, and close union with God; for he gives most who gives with joy, and God loves a cheerful giver. (Mother Teresa, *Jesus*, p. 111)

Joy must be one of the pivots of our life. (Mother Teresa, *Heart of Joy*, p. 127)

## Reflection

For Mother Teresa, joy was a gift of the Holy Spirit, a mark of the Reign of God, our Lady's strength, Mother Teresa's own strength, and her sisters' and brothers' strength. Joy was prayer, love, gratitude to God, and intimate and constant union with God. Joy was the way for her and her followers to preach the Gospel. A person who is overflowing with joy is a reflection of God's love, a witness for the hope of eternal happiness, and a preacher without words.

Mother Teresa enjoyed traveling, particularly because it gave her ample opportunity for prayer and also for quiet conversation with people. Travelers who recognized her were eager to come and spend a few minutes with her. Just to say hello. Just to feel in the presence of an exceptional person—a saint. Just to see how a saint looked. She would ask them how they were doing, how their families and friends were, and so on. She would encourage them and promise to pray for them. She would sow kindness, joy, and trust in God. She would do another "something beautiful for God" and add another note to her wonderful symphony to God's glory. She would practice the ministry of joy.

Mother Teresa's genuine joy was a striking contrast with the lack of joy that she found in the most developed nations:

> Each time I go to Europe and America, I am struck by the unhappiness of so many people living in those rich countries: so many broken homes; children not looked after by their parents. Their first duty is to work among their own people, bring together separated couples, build good homes where the children may receive their parents' love.
>
> They have material wealth; they lack spiritual values. (Mother Teresa, *My Life*, p. 112)

Joy was also an essential part of her sisters' mission. Mother Teresa would tell them: "Joy is a need and a power for us, even physically. A Sister who has cultivated a spirit of joy feels less tired and is always ready to go doing good. A Sister filled with joy preaches without preaching. A joyful Sister is like the sunshine of God's love, the hope of eternal happiness, the flame of burning love" (Mother Teresa, *Jesus*, pp. 124–125). And to everyone, especially to her sisters, she would say: "Let no one ever come to you without coming away better and happier. . . . To children, to the poor, to all who suffer and are lonely, give always a happy smile—give them not only your care, but also your heart" (Mother Teresa, *Something Beautiful*, p. 50).

Malcolm Muggeridge, an articulate observer who encountered Mother Teresa through a BBC assignment, attested clearly to the joy of the sisters: "Their life is tough and austere by worldly standards, certainly; yet I never met such delightful, happy women, or such an atmosphere of joy as they create" (Mother Teresa, *Something Beautiful*, p. 37).

The secret of this radiating joy can be found in Mother Teresa's answer to a question about the girls who came to her and devoted "all their time and energy and life to the service of the poor":

That is what they want to give. They want to give to God everything. They know very well that it's to Christ the hungry and Christ the naked and Christ the homeless that they are doing it. And this conviction and this love is what makes the giving a joy. That's why you see the Sisters are very happy. They are not forced to be happy; they are naturally happy because they feel that they have found what they have looked for. (P. 80)

Real joy does not just happen. There is a degree of correlation between the world we create and how happy we are. Nevertheless, changing the circumstances of our life, such as our partner, job, or location, or counting on pleasures, drugs, drinking, or eating—although they can give a certain temporary relief—does not necessarily lead to a profound and satisfying joy. The secret of real joy goes deeper than just superficial circumstances. The secret of real joy is rooted in the belief that our own existence is part of a larger existence and that a certain spiritual path and philosophy of life are necessary to give our life a purpose. It is in the pursuit of that purpose that our life becomes joyful.

Real joy is perhaps the most powerful drive in the human psyche. It enhances the ability to love and be loved. It awakens the gift of aliveness. It makes every moment of our life more fresh and more creative. It puts us in touch with our deepest and true self as a child of God. It makes us listen to our own call and our inner voice that knows what we must do to get the most from our life. It converts us from a receiver to a giver.

Immediate self-gratification is disappointing. The real thing takes time. The real source of joy lies within our true self, not in the accumulation of wealth outside our self. Only from that true self, where the Trinity dwells, and where love is the rule, can emerge a genuine concern for others and a desire to make of this world a better place. That concern and desire allows us to make a greater contribution to others and to the world. It turns our eyes, hearts, minds, and hands to other people and to world problems, heralding a more compassionate and understanding era of human relationships. Real joy is a by-product of that process.

Noble purpose and noble journey! This is the way of real joy. Such joy is a mark of the loving presence of God within us that is shared with others. "Rejoice in the Lord always" (Philippians 4:4), recommended Saint Paul. This is the fullness of life. Mother Teresa reminds us that one is happy when one finds what one is looking for. One is happy in God.

✧  Have you faced disappointments? If so, how did you deal with them? What did you learn from them?

✧  How can you create joy even if you do not have the job you want or even when things are not working out?

✧  Do you have all the energy you want?

✧  Do you laugh often?

✧  Have you ever felt a deep joy in your life? If so, when? Why?

✧  Saint Augustine said to God, "You have made us and drawn us to yourself, and our heart is unquiet until it rests in you" (Augustine, p. 39). Have you experienced a restless heart? Have you found the peace of resting in God? Is there joy in such peace?

✧  Does your life have meaning and purpose? Discuss this issue in a journal entry.

✧  Do you enjoy contributing to the lives of others? What did you do for others today?

✧  Go for a walk. Enjoy the outdoors. Focus on God's loving presence within you, above you, below you, around you, everywhere. Repeat often, "God is my joy."

# God's Word

You show me the path of life.
    In your presence there is fullness of joy;
    in your right hand are pleasures forevermore.

(Psalm 16:11)

Then I will go to the altar of God,
    to God my exceeding joy;
and I will praise you with the harp,
    O God, my God.

(Psalm 43:4)

I will see you again, and your hearts will rejoice, and no one will take your joy from you. (John 16:22)

Rejoice in the Lord always; again I will say, Rejoice. (Philippians 4:4)

I will greatly rejoice in the LORD,
    my whole being shall exult in my God.

(Isaiah 61:10)

**Closing prayer:** I beg you, dear God, come and make your dwelling in me so that I can be fully alive and live life to the fullest, with the greatest joy. Let my joy be my prayer of gratitude to you.

## ✧ **Meditation 9** ✧

# Trust in God

**Theme:** Mother Teresa said, "Trust in the good God who loves us, who cares for us, who sees all, knows all, can do all things for my good and the good of souls" (Mother Teresa, *Jesus*, p. 39).

**Opening prayer:** Dear God, I have no way to know whether I am on the side of truth or on my way to you, except by putting my complete trust in you and by doing things your way. Grant me the grace to decipher your presence here and now, and to be able to say at every event and turn of my life, "It is the Lord!" (John 21:7).

## About Mother Teresa

Mother Teresa liked to demonstrate how divine providence works and how much she trusted God, by telling this story about her mission in Calcutta:

> We cook for nine thousand people every day. One day one sister came and said, "Mother, there's nothing to eat, nothing to give to the people." I had no answer. And then by nine o'clock that morning a truck full of bread came to our house. The government gives a slice of bread and milk each day to the poor children. That day—no one in the city knew why—but suddenly all the schools were

closed. And all the bread came to Mother Teresa. See, God closed the schools. He would not let our people go without food. And this was the first time, I think, in their lives that they had had such good bread and so much. This way you can see the tenderness of God. (Neff, p. 163)

José Luis González-Balado, who had known Mother Teresa since 1969 and authored several books on her, wrote:

Many people believe that the global reality Mother Teresa called Providence acts by secondary causes. In other words, God usually makes use of people.

For example, instead of miraculously filling the sisters' pantry, clothing racks, or medicine chest during the night, God softly awakens a giving heart in people of generous means, often when these people have more than enough. (P. 141)

González-Balado explains that, for example, when someone donates a truckload of food to Mother Teresa's soup kitchen, the truck driver will likely be inspired to refuse his customary tip for unloading it. He adds that Mother Teresa will sign the truck driver's invoice and file it—not so that she will know who to ask for another donation, but so that she can thank the donor and ask God to reward him or her.

**Pause:** As Jesus suggested, look at the birds of the sky and consider the flowers of the field (see Matthew 6:26–28). What role does Providence play in your life?

## Mother Teresa's Words

Trust God.
>Feel the security of divine providence.
>Trust him.
>He knows.
>He will provide.
>Let him test and trust our faith in him.
>Wait on him.
>Trust and believe.

(Mother Teresa, *My Life*, p. 110)

Money? I never give it a thought. It always comes. We do all our work for our Lord; he must look after us. If he wants something to be done, he must give us the means. If he does not provide us with the means, then it shows that he does not want that particular work. I forget about it. (Mother Teresa, *My Life*, p. 112)

Concerning the economic means for supporting our works of charity, we live by the words of Jesus. He said, "the Father cares for you and knows your needs. In his eyes, you are more important than the lilies of the field or the birds of the sky" (see Mt 6:26–34).

We have never had to reject anyone for lack of resources. The good God has always shown the most delicate care and a love full of tenderness for the poor, using us to offer them out of the abundance of his love. (Mother Teresa, *Heart of Joy*, pp. 122–123)

# Reflection

When she decided to leave behind a happy life as a missionary sister of Our Lady of Loreto, Mother Teresa committed a great act of trust in divine providence. She knew that she had to go where God was calling her, but she did not know how to get there. She had no financial support. She had no clear idea how things were going to work out. Uncertainty and unpredictability were her lot. "I was on the street," she recalled, "with no shelter, no company, no helper, no money, no employment, no promise, no guarantee, no security" (Mother Teresa, *My Life*, p. 10).

As the order grew, Mother Teresa and her sisters received no salary and did not ask for money, for themselves or even for the poor people they served. They accomplished their work through the pure love of God. And somehow what was needed was always there. God was the provider. Mother Teresa believed that if God wanted the work she was doing, God would send the means; if God did not send the means, that showed that God did not want the project in the first place. Money was not a problem. It poured in for every project. Her faith in her calling as well as her complete trust in God never faltered.

As Abraham believed in the Promise of God and obeyed God even by accepting God's command for him to sacrifice his own son, and as the Virgin Mary (whose faith was her greatest merit) believed, Mother Teresa believed in the call of God and trusted God and had faith that God would not let her down. In that spirit, she lived all her life. That is why she was able to make wonders.

To illustrate how divine providence worked with her, Mother Teresa recalled: "One time we had picked up a man for whom a rare medicine was needed. While we were wondering how we could get it, a man knocked at our door with an abundant sampler of medicines. Among them was the one we urgently needed" (Mother Teresa, *Heart of Joy*, p. 43).

Mother Teresa described her philosophy about Providence directly and boldly:

> We have no income, no government grant, no church maintenance: only divine providence.
>
> We have dealt with thousands and thousands of poor, but we never had to send anybody away because we had nothing to give. There is always something. Jesus keeps his word: we are more important to his Father than the flowers and the grass and the birds. (Mother Teresa, *My Life*, p. 61)

The Missionaries of Charity learned from Mother Teresa a sense of adventure. They were able to go anyplace without fear if doing so meant furthering their mission—even to a violent area in the south Bronx. Mother Teresa said:

> In New York, in the area where we live, conflict, suffering, and hate abound. Nevertheless, the Sisters go about wherever they wish without anyone doing them the least bit of harm. Our sari is for the people a sign of our consecration to God, that we belong to him. The rosary that we carry in our hand is a great protection, a defense, a help. (González-Balado, p. 31)

"Go forth" (see Genesis 12:1) was God's first word to Abraham. God's word was a challenge to Abraham. Abraham did not understand. He was unable to grasp the where, why, and how of his going. He had neither map nor direction nor name of destination. Yet, the call was clear: "Go forth." In other words: "I am God, trust me. I'll be with you. I'll get you there. Take a risk. Leave everything behind and go." And Abraham left. He became our father in faith and the pioneer of trust in God. It takes much courage to venture with God. But when we do that, and only then, things fall in place and we begin to see the meaning of all events. ·

The irony of trust is that if we trust only in our own intelligence, strength, and personality, we will fail. To place our trust in such things leads to frustration and despair. We cannot be totally free until we live in trust in God. Then we can afford to live even in poverty, as the poorest of the poor, having nothing, clinging to nothing, for we possess all that we really want.

When we learn to abandon ourselves to divine providence, we have everything we hope for. Trust makes wonders. The birds of the sky and the flowers of the field are miracles of trust. When we seek first heaven, all material needs are taken care of, for our God proves to have been the faithful God all along (see Deuteronomy 7:9; Isaiah 49:7; 2 Thessalonians 3:3; 1 John 1:9). If we abandon ourselves to God's providence, God will never abandon us. Mother Teresa did just that.

✧ Everyone needs an essential person to trust—a spouse, a relative, a friend. Who is the most trusted person in your life? Have you ever trusted Jesus Christ as a friend?

✧ We know we can lose our job, our money, and our valued relationships. Do you usually feel worried, insecure, and sleepless? Why or why not?

✧ "The LORD said to [Abraham]: 'Go from your country and your kindred and your father's house to the land that I will show you. . . .'" So [Abraham] went, as the LORD had told him" (Genesis 12:1–4). Are you able to trust God and take a risk if God's call for you requires that you travel without a map? Write a dialogue with God about this issue.

✧ Suppose that as you leave the post office, you meet a man with a microphone who wants to interview you for a TV program. How do you answer his two questions: "Does Jesus Christ make a difference in your life? Does the faithfulness of God, being at the center of all, have some practical consequences in your daily experiences?"

✧ Pray repeatedly, "I put my trust in God."

# God's Word

Look at the birds of the air; they neither sow nor reap nor gather into barns, and yet your heavenly Father feeds them. Are you not of more value than they? And can any of you by worrying add a single hour to your span of life? And why do you worry about clothing? Consider the lilies of the field, how they grow; they neither toil nor spin, yet I tell you, even Solomon in all his glory was not clothed like one of these. But if God so clothes the grass of the field, which is alive today and tomorrow is thrown into the oven, will he not much more clothe you—you of little faith? (Matthew 6:26–30)

**Closing prayer:** "My God, you, only you. I trust in your call, your inspiration. You will not let me down" (Mother Teresa, *My Life,* p. 10).

✧ **Meditation 10** ✧

# Family Life

**Theme:** Mother Teresa advised, "We must make our home like a second 'Nazareth' where Jesus can come and live with us" (Mother Teresa, *One Heart*, p. 22).

**Opening prayer:** Lord, make of my family a united, peaceful, and holy family, so that we—every one of us—can be fulfilled and can grow together Godward. Lord, make my family your family, and make our house your home. Please, Lord, come and live with us.

## About Mother Teresa

A sixty-six-year-old Hungarian doctor, who was married and the father of seven grown and settled children, came to Calcutta to work with Mother Teresa. He was convinced that he was called to devote himself to the poor. Mother Teresa did not know him. She told him to pray about his new vocation and assigned him to work with her patients. After a while, he asked Mother Teresa if he could stay. She told him that she had prayed about it and decided to accept him. He was happy to learn that. But she asked him to go home and to bring his wife back with him, as she could help also. Mother Teresa's main concern was for his family. She did not want him to break his family ties even for the sake of the poor.

Mother Teresa insisted on the necessity of unity, love, joy, and peace in family life. For purposes of illustration, she did not hesitate to recall her own family:

> I cannot forget my mother. She was usually very busy all day long. But when sunset drew near, it was her custom to hurry with her tasks in order to be ready to receive my father.
>
> At the time we did not understand, and we would smile and even joke a little about it. Today I cannot help but call to mind that great delicacy of love that she had for him. No matter what happened, she was always prepared, with a smile on her lips, to welcome him.
>
> Today we have no time. Fathers and mothers are so busy that when children come home they are not welcomed with love or with a smile. (Neff, p. 252)

**Pause:** Do you make time for your father, mother, husband, wife, children, and other family members?

## Mother Teresa's Words

Holiness starts in the home, by loving God and those around us for his sake. (Mother Teresa, *My Life*, p. 46)

A family that prays together stays together. (Mother Teresa, *Heart of Joy*, p. 37)

Today there is so much trouble in the world and I think that much of it begins at home. The world is suffering so much because there is no peace. There is no peace because there is no peace in the family and we have so many thousands and thousands of broken homes. (Mother Teresa, *Life in the Spirit*, p. 71)

How many times does a child run away from home because there is no one there to love him! How often it is that the elderly in the family are not at home. Instead, they are in nursing homes because no one has time for them. The poor are right in your own homes. Are you aware of that? (Mother Teresa, *One Heart*, p. 21)

# Reflection

Mother Teresa was an adamant advocate for the family. She considered the family unit a sacred creation. She never ceased teaching that "love begins at home" and "the sorrows of the world have their origin in the family" (Mother Teresa, *Heart of Joy*, p. 33). She also never ceased teaching that "much restlessness and suffering start with the family. The family today is becoming less united, is not praying together, is not sharing happiness, is beginning to fall apart" (p. 52).

Her convictions about family life went back to her Christian tenets as well as to her own family. All the members of her family, especially after the death of her father, were united and tried always to live for one another and make one another happy. Her mother knew how to raise her children in the love of God and in love for their neighbor. She was a holy woman who wanted to make her family holy.

Mother Teresa insisted much on the dignity of woman, on the important role of mother, and on the functions and vocations that God had confided to woman. She liked to tell the following story to illustrate how important a mother is for a child:

> The home is where the mother is. Once I picked up a child and took him to our children's home, gave him a bath, clean clothes, everything, but after a day the child ran away. He was found again by somebody else but again he ran away. Then I said to the Sisters: "Please follow that child. One of you stay with him and see where he goes when he runs away." And the child ran away a third time. There under a tree was the mother. She had put two stones under a small earthenware vessel and was cooking something that she had picked up from the dustbins. The Sister asked the child: "Why did you run away from the home?" And the child said: "But this is my home because this is where my mother is."
>
> Mother was there. That was home. That the food was taken from the dustbins was all right because mother had cooked it. It was mother that hugged the child, mother who wanted the child and the child had its mother.

Between a wife and a husband it is the same." (Mother Teresa, *Life in the Spirit*, pp. 72–73)

Mother Teresa was convinced that

> all over the world there is so much suffering because the family is destroyed! It is the woman who guards the family's love and unity.
>
> Every woman can be equal to men if we have brains and if we have money. But no man can become equal to women in love and in ability to show service. (Mother Teresa, *My Life*, p. 77)

Mother Teresa was also tenaciously outspoken against abortion: "Abortion has become the greatest destroyer of peace. It destroys love. It destroys the image of God. It destroys the presence of God. It destroys the conscience of the mother" (Mother Teresa, *Loving Jesus*, p. 14). Whenever she was invited to speak, she would remind everyone that abortion is a crime against children, women, family, and life. Even at the ceremony where she was awarded the Nobel Prize for peace, she spoke out and condemned abortion as the greatest of crimes. She always courageously said what was important to her, even if some people in her audience might have had different opinions.

Mother Teresa's conviction as a defender of life was so strong that she openly criticized acceptance of abortion in the most powerful nations of the world:

> It is very painful to accept what is happening in Western countries: a child is destroyed by the fear of having too many children and having to feed it or to educate it.
>
> I think they are the poorest people in the world, who do an act like that.
>
> A child is a gift of God.
>
> I feel that the poorest country is the country that has to kill the unborn child to be able to have extra things and extra pleasures. They are afraid to have to feed one more child! (Mother Teresa, *My Life*, p. 63)

She concluded, "Life belongs to God, and we have no right to destroy it" (Mother Teresa, *Heart of Joy*, p. 66).

Besides love, understanding, mutual help, and striving for a continuing unity in the family, one other tool for sustaining family ties was dear to Mother Teresa. She summarized it in seven golden words: "The family that prays together, stays together" (Mother Teresa, *Loving Jesus,* p. 14). Prayer can help to make the house another Nazareth where love, peace, joy, unity, and mutual help and support reign.

The Christian family is meant to be the image of the Holy Trinity. The communion that bonds a husband, a wife, and children invokes the communion of the Father and the Son in the Holy Spirit. The affinity of feelings, affections, concerns, and interests that unites all the members of the family in fulfilling one another witnesses God's love, the great love of total loyalty and commitment. In love, partners affirm the unity that creates new life for themselves, for their children, and for all who will see them grow in being what is best for each.

Saint Paul said: "See that none of you repays evil for evil, but always seek to do good to one another and to all. Rejoice always, pray without ceasing, give thanks in all circumstances; for this is the will of God in Christ Jesus for you. Do not quench the Spirit" (1 Thessalonians 5:15–19). This is the vocation of Christians and especially of those who live the commitment of family life. They are not to suppress the Spirit, but to detect the life-giving Spirit, who is at the center of their togetherness. And that is why Saint Paul said also, "I bow my knees before the Father, from whom every family in heaven and on earth takes its name" (Ephesians 3:14–15).

A family life is a distinctive setting for practicing integrity, trust, faithfulness, care, mutual support, and spiritual and emotional growth, and especially for experiencing God's disclosure and presence. "Holiness," said Mother Teresa, "starts in the home" (Mother Teresa, *My Life,* p. 46).

✧ Can you see your family life, in its depth, as a context for the presence of God in its midst? Why or why not?

✧ Is holiness the monopoly of faithful popes, bishops, priests, monks, nuns, and very special people? In what ways can holiness be extended to a married couple? To an entire family? To family life? In what ways can holiness be a common family endeavor?

✧ Do you cherish family meals and festive parties like Christmas and birthday celebrations? How does your family celebrate Christmas, Lent, Easter, and Pentecost? Do you participate joyfully in dinner conversations? Do the members of your family talk to one another? Do they listen to one another? What steps might you take to improve this aspect of family life?

✧ Does your family worship together and spend time together? What are your times of family prayer?

✧ Does your family read the Scriptures together, and meditate, and pray? If so, who reads? Who listens? At what time do you do this?

✧ What can you do this week to show more love to your family? Make a list, act on it, and at the end of a week, review your success.

✧ You may know some families dealing with shaky marriages, questions of divorce, unexpected teenage pregnancies, single-parent situations, parent-child conflicts, sickness, drugs, alcohol, aging, and death. What can you do to give hope to a broken family, to help make its members whole and holy?

✧ When is communication in your family at its best? How do you handle differences when they occur?

✧ Does your family have a common concern for peace, reconciliation, justice, the poor, and the hungry? If so, how do you express this concern?

## God's Word

[Jesus] went down with [his parents] and came to Nazareth, and was obedient to them. (Luke 2:51)

A man leaves his father and his mother and clings to his wife, and they become one flesh. (Genesis 2:24)

So God created humankind in his image,
    in the image of God he created them;
    male and female he created them.
God blessed them, and God said to them, "Be fruitful and multiply." (Genesis 1:27–28)

Honor your father and mother. (Mark 10:19; see also Exodus 20:12)

No city or house divided against itself will stand. (Matthew 12:25)

**Closing prayer:**

Dear God of Joy,
Give me the grace to make my home another Nazareth where peace, love, and happiness reign. Let me love You through the love that is given to my family.

Let my mission of love begin in my own home, and then spread out to all who are in need of Your love and grace. Let Your love take root first in my heart and then in the hearts of all those with whom I come into contact.

Let my home be a center of kindness, compassion, and mercy. Give me the grace to make anyone who comes into contact with me go away better and happier.

Let the love I have given others, even in small ways, come back to me as Your grace. Let me forgive always and grant that this forgiveness will return to me and flourish.

Let me begin then in the place where I am, with the people I know, and let the lamp of Your love always shine in the windows of my heart and my home. Amen. (Egan, *At Prayer*, p. 77)

✧  **Meditation 11**  ✧

# Leadership

**Theme:** The most effective leaders are those who serve their followers.

**Opening prayer:** Dear God, help me to understand that leadership means not drawing others to do what I say, but doing what you say, and serving those who are supposed to follow.

## About Mother Teresa

When Javier Perez de Cuellar, the secretary general of the United Nations, introduced Mother Teresa to the audience of the General Assembly Hall with the words, "I present to you the most powerful woman in the world" (Le Joly, *Mother Teresa*, p. 29), he drew everyone's attention to her extraordinary leadership.

Besides founding and leading the thousands of members of the Missionaries of Charity and the Co-Workers, and all their works worldwide, she knew her way around and how to get what she needed for her poor. People trusted her, and she contacted many leaders, both civilian and religious, when she needed to do so. It did not take much time, for example, for her to obtain a free house for AIDS patients in New York; Mother Teresa walked right into the offices of the mayor and governor of New York and received what she wanted. She telephoned President Reagan when she needed food for the starving people of Ethiopia. She went straight to the president of Bangladesh and convinced him to intervene to help the sisters who were in trouble there. She persuaded the queen of Spain to pray with her when a house for the sisters was opened in Madrid. The pope counted on her interventions many times.

In one peculiar meeting, this saintly Catholic nun had to convince the communist president of Cuba to allow the sisters to open a house to serve the poor people in his country. "Well, here, after the Revolution, the class of poor people no longer exists," Fidel Castro informed her. Mother Teresa said that was fine, but she and her sisters would also serve the children and old people who had been abandoned and neglected, the alcoholics, and the former prisoners. To that Castro responded: "Ah, well, then. Come, Mother. The Revolution and the Cuban people welcome you" (González-Balado, pp. 119–120).

Her great love and her focus on Jesus Christ were so central to the life, career, and leadership of this "most powerful woman in the world" that she could win over even the leader of a nation in which atheism is the official doctrine. Fr. Edward Le Joly, SJ, who knew her from the beginning of the Missionaries of Charity, attested to that as follows:

> Mother is a great energizer truly indefatigable. Her charismatic influence is able to galvanize people into working with her and spreading her ideas and ideals. She has all the qualities of a leader: decision, a clear aim, a plan of action, speed in executing it. She has the capacity to gather and form a team around herself, to fill its members with enthusiasm, and get them to do things they did not think themselves capable of doing. She never delays, postpones, procrastinates. For her the work of the Lord, the service of God's poor people, brooks no delay. These qualities were not acquired, but given by God to fit her for the task he would entrust to her.
>
> . . . Her Sisters listen to her, look up to her, accept whatever she says in a spirit of faith. . . .

She has a single aim and purpose: the glory of Jesus to be procured through the sanctification of as many persons as possible. Jesus comes first, all is for him: "We do it for Jesus" sums up all her activity. "We do it for Jesus, with Jesus, to Jesus, by Jesus, in Jesus. We see him in our needy neighbor. We must love as Jesus did, namely without measure, without second thoughts, without desire for reward." (Le Joly, *Mother Teresa*, p. 80)

**Pause:** When you have the opportunity to be a leader, how do you approach the task?

## Mother Teresa's Words

Formation will be given not so much by words, but by the living example of those in charge of formation, as well as of each one in the community, and also by prayer, sacrifice, and real personal concern for them preparing the way for the Lord in their lives. (Mother Teresa, *Jesus*, p. 115)

The essential thing is not what we say but what God says to us and through us. (Mother Teresa, *Life in the Spirit*, p. 20)

We [Mother Teresa and her sisters] do not intend to impose our faith on others. We only expect Christ to reach out with his light and his life in and through us, to the world of misery. We expect the poor, no matter what their beliefs are, to feel drawn toward Christ as they see us and to invite us to get closer to them, to enter their lives. (Mother Teresa, *Heart of Joy*, p. 46)

## Reflection

All the customary qualities that contribute to making a world leader—such as power, wealth, fame, a cunning mind, politics, education, and connections—do not necessarily make a Christian leader. Those things may even be irrelevant.

The first requirement for a Christian leader is, paradoxically, to allow himself or herself to be led rather than to lead. A Christian leader is supposed to be poor in spirit, open to God, vulnerable, and willing to be a vehicle for God to others. A Christian leader is concerned with drawing others to God, not to himself or herself. Being popular, taking a stand according to the latest polls, and even performing the most beautiful rites and ceremonies are not of primary interest. What comes first is the quality of the answer to Jesus Christ's question, "Do you love me?" (John 21:15–17). Jesus repeated this question to Peter, the first leader of the church, three times because it points to the most relevant quality that makes a leader a Christian leader. If the answer is yes, then Jesus Christ directs the leader to tend and feed his lambs and sheep—for us, that means building hospitals, taking care of the poor and the dying, and all other acts of mercy.

Mother Teresa did exactly those things. Whatever she did for others, she did it for Jesus Christ. She was convinced that Jesus Christ wants us to be faithful before we are successful.

With this attitude in mind, heart, and action, a Christian leader cannot fail, because God cannot fail. A Christian leader yields the command to God.

Mother Teresa, the little, poor nun who was not a head of state, who had no money, no castles, no worldly credentials of any kind, reached an eminent point in leadership. Why? Because she became a servant role model by truly epitomizing Jesus Christ's message, which was To be first and great, one has to be the servant of all. Because she took the lowest seat at the feast, God exalted her to a leadership seat of high esteem—one that a person cannot earn or learn, but can only receive from above.

Mother Teresa was always open to God's inspiration and always ready to obey God's will. When she was traveling by train to Darjeeling for a spiritual retreat and received her special "call within a call," she perceived God's will for her and she obeyed. Mother Teresa, like many other great leaders who recognize their own limitations, weaknesses, and inadequacies, looked constantly to God for answers and solutions. She was close to the One who said, "Apart from me you can do nothing" (John 15:5), and of whom Saint Paul said, "I can do all things through him who strengthens me" (Philippians 4:13). She herself said, "The most important thing in my life has been my encounter with Christ: He is my support" (Mother Teresa, *Heart of Joy*, p. 46). With this kind of faith, she was able to move mountains (see Matthew 17:20–21).

Also, a Christian leader may convince others of God's word by preaching it or by just living it. That is what some Christian masters call preaching without preaching. Even though she spoke often to large audiences—all kinds of audiences, professors and spiritual and political leaders included—Mother Teresa was convinced that preaching by example was the best way to attract people to Jesus. She showed her convictions by the model of her life. She was true to herself at all times. To be genuine like that can help a Christian leader attract followers. Often, when one does not seek popularity, one can become immensely popular.

Genuine people do not lead by force, not even by persuasion. Genuine people lead by just being true, trustworthy, and real. They exhibit new possibilities; foster new, fulfilling dreams; create paradigm shifts; and get others to reach for something higher. In the presence of such a leader, one is truly inspired. People are transformed.

Mother Teresa knew her way to the human psyche. She never intended to cry out for changing laws. She went deeper. She wanted to reach people's consciences, minds, and hearts. Her intention was to change people who make and change laws. Then, laws and practices would become more just and more humane. A leader like this makes a difference. Mother Teresa made a difference.

Christian leaders must be people of God first. Of course, they must make a real contribution to finding solutions for individual and social problems, family conflicts, national calamities, or any other tensions nationally or internationally. But first of all and above all, they are called to let the voice of God be heard by people so that people can be consoled, can be comforted, and can grow in love. The leadership of power and control will then yield to the leadership of powerlessness, humility, and vulnerability, in which Jesus Christ becomes the original and final cause for all that we do, and love becomes the only policy. A true leader is a true lover. Mother Teresa was driven by passion for God and for all human beings. She was a true leader.

✧ If Jesus Christ looked in your eyes right now and asked you what he asked Peter, "Do you love me?" what would be your sincere answer? How can your love for Jesus Christ be a sign of leadership?

✧ A person's real success can be the result of direct obedience to God. Do you feel that God's will and guidance are clear in your life? When God's will is clear, do you try to take the role of a leader within your family, place of work, and community?

✧ When you believe that you are following God's will, do you feel enthusiastic? Joyful? Trusting? Hopeful? Reluctant? More loving? Why? Write a poem or create a piece of artwork or music that expresses your feeling or feelings.

✧ Our choices not only affect but infect our entire environment. Many of us worship the wrong things—money, power, pleasure, fame, self, or other people. Have you thought about your fundamental choice? Do you allow God to lead you through the mountains and valleys of your life?

✧ In what areas can Mother Teresa be your heroine, role model, leader, and hope for tomorrow? Which of the following characteristics of this woman of distinctive and uncommon power has made the biggest impression on your heart, mind, and soul: her constant obedience, her tenacity, her piety, or her determination to follow Jesus?

✧ Can you name a spiritual author or a spiritual leader who impresses you? How does that person influence you?

✧ Listen to God's words:

Do not fear, for I have redeemed you.

. . . . . . . . . . . . .

When you pass through the waters, I will be with you;

and through the rivers, they shall not overwhelm
> you;
when you walk through fire you shall not be burned,
> and the flame shall not consume you.
>
> (Isaiah 43:1–2)

Do you feel comfortable giving the lead to God? Can you think of any event in which you felt as if you were drowning or being burned? God has offered to help; consider asking God to guide you through such an event, or its memory. You may want to write a dialogue exploring this issue.

✧ Do you know your talents and gifts? Reflect on a skill you have. What things, great or small, do you like to do? Can you touch a life through a talent of yours? Are you able to draw someone to God through your words and especially your deeds?

## God's Word

Whoever wishes to be great among you must be your servant. (Matthew 20:26)

I am the good shepherd. The good shepherd lays down his life for the sheep. (John 10:11)

Where there is no guidance, a nation falls,
> but in an abundance of counselors there is safety.
>
> (Proverbs 11:14)

**Closing prayer:** "Lord, you know everything; you know that I love you" (John 21:17). And, led by your light, I ask you to help me extend your love to all my brothers and sisters, and devotedly serve them, so that they may be drawn closer to your heart.

✧　**Meditation 12**　✧

# Peacemaking

**Theme:** The closer we are to Christ, the closer we will experience peace within ourselves, around us, and beyond. "Find Jesus, and you will find peace" (Mother Teresa, *Jesus*, p. 63), said Mother Teresa.

**Opening prayer:** Pull me, Lord, closer and closer to your heart, because I know that real peace is the fruit of my closeness to you. I love you, Lord, and I love you in my neighbors, no matter who and what they are.

## About Mother Teresa

In January 1991, Mother Teresa wrote to Presidents George Bush of the United States and Saddam Hussein of Iraq, in the hope that they would change their minds and would not go to war:

> I write to you with tears in my eyes and with the love of God in my heart, to beg you . . . with all my heart that you spare no efforts in favor of the peace of God and to reconcile yourselves with one another.
> . . . You have the capacity and force to destroy the presence and image of God, in his men, in his women, and in his children. Listen, please, to the voice of God.

God has created us to love each other with his love and not to destroy ourselves with our hates. . . .

I beg you . . . on behalf of those who will be deprived of the most precious gift which God is able to give us: life. I beg you that you save our brothers and sisters, yours and ours, because God gives them to us to love them and to care for them. We do not have the right to destroy what God has given us. Please, please: allow your intelligence to be the intelligence and will of God. You have the capacity to bring war into the world and to make peace. Please, choose the way of peace. (González-Balado, pp. 102–104)

**Pause**: Reflect on what you could contribute to peace in the world.

## Mother Teresa's Words

May we all be instruments of peace, of love, and of compassion. (Mother Teresa, *Heart of Joy*, p. 29)

Peace and war start within one's own home. If we really want peace for the world, let us start by loving one another within our families. (Mother Teresa, *Heart of Joy*, p. 90)

Let us not use bombs and guns to overcome the world. Let us use love and compassion. Peace begins with a smile—smile five times a day at someone you don't really want to smile at at all—do it for peace. So let us radiate the peace of God and so light his light and extinguish in the world and in the hearts of all men all hatred and love for power. (Mother Teresa, *Life in the Spirit*, p. 85)

## Reflection

The day 17 October 1979 was an interesting and special one in the life of Mother Teresa. On that day, the news that she had won the Nobel Prize for peace was quickly spread to every corner of the world. And many who had not known about this ordinary woman started to realize how extraordinary she was.

The committee of Norway applauded Mother Teresa not only because her work was worthy of the prize but because by receiving the award, she gave honor to it. Needless to say, the entire amount of money that came with it was immediately directed to the poor.

Another great day was 26 October 1985, when Mother Teresa came to the United Nations. She was introduced by Secretary-General Javier Perez de Cuellar as the most powerful woman on earth. He also said: "She is the United Nations! She is the peace of the world!" (González-Balado, p. 98). But Mother Teresa quickly moved to focus on her mission, suggesting that the gathering thank God for allowing the United Nations to do its work for peace and pointing out that abortion destroys peace.

A spiritual friendship developed between Mother Teresa and Pope John Paul II. On many occasions, the pope asked her to contribute to his campaigns for peace, prayer, holiness of the family, the unborn child's right to life, and the union of all Christians. Mother Teresa was glad to contribute to all that.

Even though all these events were great works for peace, her favorite contribution was her daily work for the poor, the hungry, and the dying. She was absolutely convinced that what she did for others was at the same time a work for peace. She put it clearly this way: "Our works of love are nothing but the works of peace" (Mother Teresa, *Life in the Spirit*, p. 85).

The example and goal in all of Mother Teresa's actions was Jesus Christ. Jesus Christ broke down the wall of hostility between Jews and Gentiles. And by doing so, he also abolished the ideological, nationalistic, and militaristic barriers between nations, as well as racial, economic, social, and other class and personal barriers between individuals. Saint Paul reminds us: "There is no longer Jew or Greek, there is no longer slave or free, there is no longer male or female; for all of you are one in Christ Jesus" (Galatians 3:28).

Mother Teresa, too, cared for everyone regardless of their beliefs, race, nationality, social status, and differences. She treated all people as children of God, saw Jesus Christ in every one of them, and saw everyone as Jesus Christ himself. More-

over, Jesus Christ is not something added to our humanness.
Jesus Christ, by virtue of the Incarnation, became our very humanness—our true selves. When the law of Christ is our law,
peace becomes not only possible but certain. The law of Christ
is the law of peace.

✧ Jesus commanded, "Love your enemies" (Luke 6:27).
Is it possible to obey that commandment when war is going
on between your country and another country, or between
you and another person?

✧ Do you have enemies? If so, who are they? How do
you deal with them?

✧ Do you think wars result from social, economic, psychological, or spiritual causes? Give reasons for your answer.

✧ Compare the seven deadly sins (pride, covetousness,
lust, anger, gluttony, envy, and sloth) with the seven virtues
(faith, hope, love, prudence, justice, temperance, and forti-
tude). How do those sins and virtues affect your work toward
peace within yourself and with others?

✧ Choose a country you know nothing about. Go to the
library or the Internet and learn about it. Tell your family and
friends what you discover. Be the country's good ambassador
for some time.

✧ How can you affect someone positively today?

✧ For a week or two, find positive things to do for other
people. Do them out of love, without expecting a return favor.
Visit someone who is sick. Call someone who is lonely. Provide a dinner for someone who is hungry. Write a letter to a
forgotten friend. Do at least one thing a day.

✧ Read Matthew 25:31–46. Can it be a lesson for making
peace with others?

✧ Repeat the phrase, "Peace be with you," several times. Try to make it a usual greeting when you meet or leave others.

## God's Word

Peace I leave with you; my peace I give to you. (John 14:27)

Let the peace of Christ rule in your hearts, to which indeed you were called in the one body. (Colossians 3:15)

**Closing prayer:** Dear God, let the cup of violence, anguish, desolation, and uncertainty pass me by. Do not allow me to deceive others, but bless me with your gifts of truth, joy, love, and peace. Keep me close to you. Then, I will be closer to others. You are my peace.

## ✧ **Meditation 13** ✧

# Instrumentality

**Theme:** Being "a pencil" in God's hands (González-Balado, p. 23), as Mother Teresa called herself, is, in Christian life, a total act of surrender to God.

**Opening prayer:**

Lord, make me an instrument of your peace.
Where there is hatred, let me sow love;
    where there is injury, pardon;
    where there is doubt, faith;
    where there is despair, hope;
    where there is darkness, light;
    where there is sadness, joy.
O divine Master, grant that I may not so much seek
    to be consoled, as to console;
    to be understood, as to understand;
    to be loved, as to love.
For it is in giving that we receive;
    it is in pardoning that we are pardoned;
    it is in dying that we are born to eternal life.

(Neff, p. 58)

This prayer of Saint Francis was incorporated in the daily devotions of the Missionaries of Charity and repeated often by audiences to which Mother Teresa was invited to speak.

## About Mother Teresa

Mother Teresa loved the following prayer, written by John Henry Newman, a nineteenth-century English theologian and cardinal. The Missionaries of Charity pray it together after mass.

> Dear Lord, help me to spread your fragrance wherever I go. Flood my soul with your spirit and life. Penetrate and possess my whole being so utterly that all my life may only be a radiance of yours.
>
> Shine through me, and be so in me that every soul I come in contact with may feel your presence in my soul. Let them look up and see no longer me, but only you, O Lord! Stay with me, then I shall begin to shine as you do; so to shine as to be a light to others. The light, O Lord, will be all from you; none of it will be mine; it will be you shining on others through me. Let me thus praise you in the way you love best, by shining on those around me.
>
> Let me preach you without preaching, not by words but by my example, by the catching force, the sympathetic influence of what I do, the evident fullness of the love my heart bears to you. Amen. (Neff, p. 91)

Mother Teresa did not preach about Jesus Christ very often. Her life was the best speech, because she lived in a way that reminds others of Christ. By seeing her way of life, one is drawn to Christ. When she said, "Those who see us will see Christ in us" (p. 95), she meant it. She illustrated her belief with the story of a man who was profoundly touched by the sisters and transformed:

> One day, we picked up a man off the street who looked like a fairly well-to-do person. He was completely drunk. He couldn't even stand up because he was so drunk!
>
> We took him to our home. The sisters treated him with such love, such care, such kindness.
>
> After a fortnight, he told the sisters, "Sisters, my heart is open. Through you I have come to realize that God loves me. I've felt his tender love for me. I want to go home." And we helped him get ready to go home.

After a month, he came back to our home and gave the sisters his first paycheck. He told the sisters, "Do to others what you have done to me." And he walked away a different person. (P. 100)

**Pause:** How can people know that someone is Christ's disciple? Do people know that you are Christ's follower by just looking at the way you live?

## Mother Teresa's Words

Our work is Christ's work, and so we have to be his instruments, to carry out our small task and to disappear. (Neff, p. 95)

We have been instrumental in preaching the Word of God to the poor, the neglected, the sorrowful, the lonely of all nations. Unworthy though we are, God has used us to make him known and loved by this God-oblivious world. (Neff, p. 98)

A Missionary of Charity is a messenger of God's love, a living lamp that offers its light to all. (Neff, p. 94)

## Reflection

Once someone has decided to follow Christ by accepting complete evangelical poverty, they extend Christ's presence by continuing his action. They become the instrument by which Christ works in this world, doing as he said: "For I have set you an example, that you also should do as I have done to you" (John 13:15) and "Just as I have loved you, you also should love one another" (John 13:34). This love, this union and communion with Christ, made the notion of instrumentality so real in the life of Mother Teresa that she was able to declare:

I do nothing of my own. He does it.

That is what I am, God's pencil. A tiny bit of pencil with which he writes what he likes. (Mother Teresa, *My Life*, pp. 101–102)

She insisted that Jesus guided her and acted through her, because people are just "carriers of God's love" (p. 14). She knew in her heart that "God writes through us, and however imperfect instruments we may be, he writes beautifully" (p. 102).

Aware of her instrumental role for Christ, Mother Teresa was always straightforward, direct, and blunt, sometimes to the point of shocking her audience, even if her audience included world leaders. She once declared at the United Nations, forcefully and without any fear or hesitation: "When we destroy an unborn child, we destroy God. We are frightened of nuclear war, we are frightened of this new disease, but we are not frightened to kill a little child. Abortion has become the great destroyer of peace" (Le Joly, *Mother Teresa*, p. 31).

Recognizing Mother Teresa's charisma, Pope John Paul II invited her to be an ambassadress-at-large to speak up openly, proclaiming the good news; defending the truth; defending the right of conscience, faith, justice, service, and worship; and preaching the crusade of the family and peace in the world. The pope also made full use of Mother Teresa's influence on people to advance his campaigns for peace, for the respect and holiness of life and the family, for prayer, for the union of all Christians, and for the revival of the values of the Gospel.

Mother Teresa saw herself as an instrument in another sense too. She did not want to be a fund-raiser, begging the rich to give money to the poor. She wanted to give "opportunity to people to love others" (Mother Teresa, *My Life*, p. 36). "Christ uses me," she said, "as an instrument to put you in touch with his poor" (Mother Teresa, *Heart of Joy*, p. 116).

God uses loving people to sanctify the world. The humbler and poorer in spirit the instrument is, the more the God of all things uses it for the realization of the Reign of God. Mother Teresa did great things because she was just "God's pencil." God made her a world figure.

✧ Ask yourself, "Am I a dark light, a false light, a bulb without the connection, having no current, therefore shedding no radiance?" (Neff, p. 93). Why or why not?

✧ Jesus said, "Let your light shine before others, so that they may see your good works and give glory to your Father in heaven" (Matthew 5:16). What steps can you take in order to shine before people in a way that will help them glorify God for what you are?

✧ Consider the gift of being made God's messenger. What reactions do you experience in that capacity—joy? Gratitude? Worry? Fear? Rebellion? Peace? Love? Share those reactions with God in prayer. Try to make your prayer a relationship with God instead of just a reflection on God.

✧ Saint John the Baptizer said, "[Jesus] must increase, but I must decrease" (John 3:30). Make a list of significant circumstances that allow Jesus Christ to increase, and you to decrease, in your own life.

✧ What does Jesus Christ's identification with others mean? How does the Lord use others as instruments for your spiritual growth? How can you improve your identification with others?

✧ Everything—God, people, pets, cars, houses, and so on—by just being, makes a statement. God makes a statement through the beauty of nature. What statement does God make through you? What is your own statement? What do you wish to say to others by the way you live?

✧ Repeat several times, "I am God's pencil."

# God's Word

You are the light of the world. A city built on a hill cannot be hid. No one after lighting a lamp puts it under the bushel basket, but on the lampstand, and it gives light to all in the house. In the same way, let your light shine before others, so that they may see your good works and give glory to your Father in heaven. (Matthew 5:14–16)

I am the vine, you are the branches. (John 15:5).

So we are ambassadors for Christ, since God is making his appeal through us. (2 Corinthians 5:20)

**Closing prayer:**

I am but an instrument of your will,
    a tool of your peace,
    a conduit of your love,
my God.

Bring me always to the place of need,
and point me always in the direction of your desire.

Be with me, God, as you were with your Son,
and let the love of Jesus Christ shine through me.

Amen.

✧  **Meditation 14**  ✧

# Devotion to Mary

**Theme:** "[Mary] can help us to love Jesus best; she is the one who can show us the shortest way to Jesus" (Neff, p. 112).

**Opening prayer:** Mary, mother of God, wrap us in your tender arms and protect us in your grace. Show us how to live God's will in humble obedience. Be with us as we serve those who bear the face of your Son in our world.

## About Mother Teresa

Mother Teresa had for our Lady deep affection and trust and great devotion. But in no way was that devotion a substitute for her complete surrender to Christ. On the contrary, it strengthened her relationship with Christ. She prayed:

> Queen of the Most Holy Rosary, in these secular times of indifference, show your power with the signs of your ancient victories, and from your throne, from which you dispense pardon and graces, mercifully regard the Church of your Son. Hasten the hour of mercy, and for me, who am the least among human beings, kneeling before you in prayer, obtain the grace I need to live righteously upon the earth. In company of all the faithful Christians throughout the world, I salute you and acclaim you as

Queen of the Most Holy Rosary. Amen. (Egan, *At Prayer*, p. 83)

From the start, the Missionaries of Charity, on the recommendation of Mother Teresa, prayed constantly for the mother of God. They displayed pictures of the Immaculate Heart of Mary or a statue of Mary in every one of their chapels and houses. Mother Teresa said: "They spread all over [Calcutta] with the rosary in hand. It is the way for us to pray with the rosary in the street; we do not go to the people without praying; the rosary has been our strength and our protection" (Mother Teresa, *My Life*, p. 43). She also said: "Now they tell me the time that it takes to reach different places by the number of rosaries they can say. When they pray as they go along, the people see it and respect them" (Egan, *At Prayer*, p. 83).

The rosary is a powerful instrument for changing people, as reported in the true story "A Gift from the Woman in White," by Barbara Bartocci. Bartocci writes that a man she calls Jim once found himself on a plane with Mother Teresa and another nun. As the passengers settled in, Mother Teresa and her companion began to pray their rosaries. For some reason, Jim, an uninspired Catholic, found himself praying along. Mother Teresa turned to look at him, and Jim was overcome with a powerful sense of peace. "Young man," she inquired, "do you say the rosary often?" "No, not really," he admitted. She dropped her rosary into his hand and said with a smile, "Well, you will now."

Months later, Jim and his wife, Ruth, found out that a friend had been diagnosed with ovarian cancer. Jim gave the friend Mother Teresa's rosary and told her the story of how it had come into his possession. "Keep it with you, Connie," he said. "It may help." After a year of surgeries, chemotherapy, and prayer, Connie returned the rosary to Jim. Her face glowed as she reported: "The tumor's gone. Completely!"

Several years passed, and Ruth's sister, Liz, suffered a divorce and then a deep depression. One day she asked Jim if she could borrow the rosary. She put it in a small velvet bag and hung it over her bedpost. At night, she simply held on to it. "I was so lonely and afraid," she later said. "Yet when I gripped the rosary, I felt as if I held a loving hand." Eventually Liz recovered and mailed the rosary back to Jim, explaining, "Someone else may need it."

One night not long after that, Ruth received a call from a stranger. This woman had heard about the rosary from a neighbor, and wondered if it might help her mother, who was in a coma, die peacefully. When the woman returned the beads a few days later, she described how her mother's face had relaxed after she told her about the beads and put them in her hand. "A few minutes later," the woman said, "she was gone."

Bartocci asks: "Is there special power in those humble beads? Or is the power of the human spirit simply renewed in each person who borrows the rosary?" She says: "Jim only knows that requests continue to come, often unexpectedly. He always responds, though whenever he lends the rosary, he says, 'When you're through needing it, send it back. Someone else may need it.'"

Bartocci explains that Jim has changed, too, since he met Mother Teresa. He discovered that she carries everything she owns in one small bag, and he now works to simplify his own life. "I try to remember what *really* counts—not money or titles or possessions, but the way we love others," he says.

**Pause:** Does devotion to our Lady have a place in your life?

## Mother Teresa's Words

The Magnificat is Our Lady's prayer of thanks. She can help us to love Jesus best; she is the one who can show us the shortest way to Jesus. Mary was the one whose intercession led Jesus to work the first miracle. "They have no wine," she said to Jesus. "Do whatever he tells you," she said to the servants. We take the part of the servants. Let us go to her with great love and trust. We are serving Jesus in the distressing disguise of the poor. (Neff, p. 112)

People like to see the sisters accompanied by Mary. With rosary in hand, they are always willing to spread the Good News. (Neff, p. 108)

# Reflection

Mother Teresa saw Mary as a model of surrender to the will of God. Mary's yes to the angel Gabriel is a profound lesson of obedience to God—the way to listen and the way to love. Also Mary is a model of Jesus' poverty, humility, kindness, thoughtfulness, and charity. Mother Teresa said:

> No one has learned so well the lesson of humility as Mary did. She, being the handmaid of the Lord, was completely empty of self, and God filled her with grace. "Full of grace" means full of God. A handmaid is at someone's disposal, to be used according to someone's wish with full trust and joy, to belong to someone without reserve. This is one main reason for the spirit of the Society. Total surrender: to be at God's disposal, to be used as it pleases him, to be his handmaid, to belong to him. (Neff, p. 104)

No one has loved Jesus as his mother did. She is an example for all those who want to love; her love was personal, intimate, understanding, trusting, generous, and meditative. Mary is a good model for contemplatives remaining in the world, like Mother Teresa and the Missionaries of Charity. That is why one can expect and understand that a devotion to Mary must be an essential part of their spirituality.

Mary had an attentive concern for the hosts of the wedding at Cana. She showed great sensitivity and thoughtfulness. She brought Jesus to manifest his power.

Mary is an example of service. Before being asked, she went to help her cousin Elizabeth with her baby.

Mary was "the most beautiful among all women, the greatest, the most humble, the purest, the holiest," "full of grace," and "the cause of our joy" (Neff, pp. 106–107). "Mary in the mystery of her annunciation and visitation is the very model of the way you should live, because first she received Jesus in her life, then she went in haste to give to her cousin Elizabeth; what she had received, she had to give. You must be like her, giving in haste the word you have received in meditation" (p. 110).

Mary is mother of God, mother of the church. She was and is mother wherever her Son was and is, collaborating with him in the salvation of the world.

Mother Teresa was absolutely convinced of the unique power of the mother of God. She always prayed to Mary, for herself and for others, and she always asked others to do the same.

Mary is the most beautiful and telling example of our relationship with Jesus Christ.

✧ Say some of the names given to our Lady, such as: Our Lady of the Lakes, Our Lady of the Snows, Our Lady of Guadalupe, Our Lady of Lourdes, Our Lady of Fátima, Notre Dame de Paris, Mother of Perpetual Help, Mother of Humankind, and Mother of Sorrows. Think about the parts of yourself you feel happy with, or the parts that need healing. Give our Lady a name that identifies the role you want her to play in you.

✧ Has the picture of Mary in your mind evolved over time? How do you see her now?

✧ Are you able to say to God, as Mary did, "Let it be with me according to your word" (Luke 1:38)?

✧ Ponder how Mary gave birth to Jesus, and how you can help extend that first Christmas to a continuous Christmas every time you give birth to Christ in someone's life.

✧ Make a resolution to visit a Marian shrine soon. There, in addition to offering traditional prayers, try to say a prayer in your own words. Thank Mary for bringing Jesus to the world and ask her to help you bring Christ to others.

✧ Pray for every expectant mother, that she may have a healthy and loved baby or babies, and that she may take care of it or them in the way Mary did Jesus.

✧ Say your favorite Marian prayer. Ponder each word of it.

## God's Word

[Mary said,] "All generations will call me blessed." (Luke 1:48)

Mary treasured all these words and pondered them in her heart. (Luke 2:19)

Standing near the cross of Jesus were his mother, and his mother's sister, Mary the wife of Clopas, and Mary Magdalene. When Jesus saw his mother and the disciple whom he loved standing beside her, he said to his mother, "Woman, here is your son." Then he said to the disciple, "Here is your mother." And from that hour the disciple took her into his own home. (John 19:25–27)

**Closing prayer:** "Silence of Mary speak to me, teach me how with you and like you I can learn to keep all things in my heart as you did, not to answer back when accused or corrected, to pray always in the silence of my heart as you did" (Neff, p. 109).

## ✧ Meditation 15 ✧

# Holiness Is for You and Me

**Theme:** "Holiness," said Mother Teresa, "is not the luxury of the few but a simple duty for you and me so let us be holy as our Father in heaven is holy" (Mother Teresa, *Life in the Spirit*, p. 24).

**Opening prayer:** "Lord, make me a saint according to your own heart, meek and humble" (p. 25).

### About Mother Teresa

Each day, before they went out into the world to do God's work on earth, Mother Teresa and her Missionaries of Charity sang the hymn of God's holiness:

> Holy, holy, holy Lord, God of power and might,
> Heaven and earth are full of your glory.
> Hosanna in the highest.
> Blessed is he who comes in the name of the Lord.
> Hosanna in the highest.
>
> (Neff, p. 146)

And Mother Teresa exhorted, "Let us in return, as an act of gratitude and adoration, determine to be holy because he is holy" (p. 146).

Mother Teresa was convinced that "holiness is a duty for all. Holiness is obtained and practiced by directing all our actions to God" (Le Joly, *Mother Teresa*, p. 125). To illustrate her point, she recalled:

> The president of Mexico sent for me. I told him that he had to become holy as a president: not a Missionary of Charity, but as a president.
> He looked at me a bit surprised, but it is like that: we have to become holy, each of us, in the place where God has put us. (Mother Teresa, *My Life*, p. 83)

Everyone can live holiness by living out this practical advice from Mother Teresa: "Give someone a smile, visit someone for a short time, make a fire for someone who is cold, read something to someone. These are small things, very small, but they will make your love for God more concrete" (Le Joly, *Mother Teresa*, p. 125).

**Pause:** What prevents you from living a holy life by just living your ordinary life with care, faith, and great love?

## Mother Teresa's Words

We have been created to be holy because we have been created in the image of God. (Mother Teresa, *My Life*, p. 75)

Holiness is not a privilege of a few but a need for all. (Mother Teresa, *Heart of Joy*, p. 47)

Holiness consists of carrying out God's will with joy. Faithfulness forges saints. (Mother Teresa, *Heart of Joy*, p. 92)

Thoughtfulness is the beginning of great sanctity. If you learn this art of being thoughtful, you will become more and more Christlike, for his heart was meek and he always thought of the needs of others—our lives to be beautiful must be full of thought for others. (Mother Teresa, *Life in the Spirit*, p. 33)

# Reflection

Mother Teresa was not only a living example for a prayerful life and union with God, she was also an advocate for holiness as everyone's responsibility—a way of life. Holiness is not an extra—something added to our life. It is an essential part of our life and the very life of lives, no matter what our own circumstances are.

Mother Teresa was holy in her own way, by being "a pencil" in God's hands. She did what was needed. She loved boundlessly the poorest of the poor. She created homes for them. She fed them. She cared for them. She healed them. She helped them eventually to die with dignity. In addition to all that, her life was full with unpredictable happenings. She had to confront continuous human tragedies resulting from accidents and disasters of both natural and human origins. Holiness is never an escape from responsibility and from participation in making a kinder and better world. She had not a minute to waste. She did not just "philosophize" about personalism and humanism, she showed us concretely what personalism and humanism meant. She was personalism and humanism in action. She was human, so human in the steps of her Master that she became for the world at large a paradigm of philanthropy. She was a model for Christian charity. She lived the Gospel's message almost literally. Unconcerned for her own well-being, she directed the entire focus of her life on the Lord Jesus Christ. She loved him in everyone. That is precisely what a saint, a holy person, does all day and all night long.

We certainly know people who do good for the sake of doing good or out of self-interest. That is not holiness. The holy is revealed when, in a moment of goodness and beauty, people open their hearts in compassion and see the Lord in what they are doing.

Mother Teresa never begged for money; she gave her audience the opportunity to do "something beautiful for God." She said: "How much you give is not important; it's how much love you put into the giving" (González-Balado, p. 116). Great love is what holiness is all about.

Saints' lives, while intriguing us, answer some of the questions we carry in the depths of our hearts and souls, such as: Why are we here? What is it all about? What is the meaning of our lives? What is the meaning of what we are doing? What is our own special assignment on this earth? Saints do ordinary things with extraordinary love. And that puzzles us.

Saints, in spite of their weaknesses, seem to be, in some way or other, a disclosure of the Holy One. The Holy One is experienced in the Holy One's power of transforming the lives of saints into witnesses of the Reign of God. The Reign is where the saints belong entirely, even with their bodies. "Do you not know that your body is a temple of the Holy Spirit within you, which you have from God, and that you are not your own? For you were bought with a price; therefore glorify God in your body" (1 Corinthians 6:19–20). Thus, they are deeply and totally involved, bodily, spiritually, and emotionally, with God's life.

Holiness emerges when our life in all its aspects of work, prayer, love, lifestyle, complexity, joy, suffering, and recreation points clearly to our origin and end, and becomes a new creation in Christ (Galatians 6:15)—a divinization in process. That is what every Christian's life is supposed to do.

Vatican Council II affirmed that all followers of Christ are asked and obligated to pursue holiness. And in the words of Thomas Merton, "Every Christian is called to follow Christ, to imitate Christ as perfectly as the circumstances of his life permit, and thereby to become a saint" (Merton, p. 34). Mother Teresa would say, "Holiness is simple duty for you and me."

✧ Ponder the meaning of the Christian life for a moment. Is it an ideology or rather a way of life? Is it understood through the mind or rather grasped through the heart? Is it a conclusion or rather an experience? Is it a set of ethical precepts or rather a relationship with the One who said, "I am the way, and the truth, and the life" (John 14:6)?

✧ Do you feel alone sometimes even though you are convinced that God is with you at all times?

✧ God is experienced in power, presence, and love. Do you feel that God has transformed your life in any way? Are you able to help someone today without expecting a favor in return?

✧ Name five holy people. Why do you think they are holy? How is the presence of God manifested in the modern world?

✧ Do you have a lot of unfinished business? Do you owe someone a long-overdue apology? Do you need to perform an act of kindness that has been postponed for too long? Does your everyday work take all your time and reduce your relationship with God to just a Sunday business? Do you usually keep your promises? How about your good resolutions? What unfinished business do you still have?

✧ Saints also have unfinished business, but they are aware of being on a journey toward God. Are you? If so, identify major crossroads, obstacles, and other features of that journey, sketching them as a timeline or map.

✧ What is your special assignment in life? What is the final meaning of your life? Is your daily life incompatible with a holy life? What can you do to make your real life a holy life? Be as specific as you can.

✧ Say in your heart many times, "Holy, holy, holy Lord."

## God's Word

You shall be holy, for I the LORD your God am holy. (Leviticus 19:2)

As God's chosen ones, holy and beloved, clothe yourselves with compassion, kindness, humility, meekness, and patience. . . . Whatever you do, in word or deed, do everything in the name of the Lord Jesus, giving thanks to God the Father through him. (Colossians 3:12–17)

**Closing prayer:** Lord, help me to take the time and to have the energy to seek to really experience you—not only talk about you—in myself, in others, and in the circumstances of my life. Let my humanness be my tangible holiness and my holiness my way of life. And let me realize that the more human I am, the more loving I become, and the more loving I am, the more holy I will be.

# J·E·S·U·S

# ✧ Works Cited ✧

Augustine, Saint. *The Works of Saint Augustine*. Book 1, *The Confessions*. Trans. Maria Boulding, ed. John E. Rotelle (Hyde Park, NY: New City Press, 1997).

Bartocci, Barbara. "A Gift from the Woman in White." Condensed from *Catholic Digest*, November 1990.

Chawla, Navin. *Mother Teresa* (Boston: Element, 1998).

Crossette, Barbara. "Pomp Pushes the Poorest from Mother Teresa's Last Rites." *New York Times International* (14 September 1997).

Egan, Eileen. *At Prayer with Mother Teresa*. Comp. and ed. Judy Bauer (Liguori, MO: Liguori Publications, 1999).

_____. *Such a Vision of the Street: Mother Teresa—the Spirit and the Work* (Garden City, NY: Doubleday and Company, 1985).

González-Balado, José Luis. *Mother Teresa: Her Life, Her Work, Her Message: A Memoir* (Liguori, MO: Liguori Publications, 1997).

Le Joly, Edward. *Mother Teresa: A Woman in Love* (Notre Dame, IN: Ave Maria Press, 1993).

_____. *Mother Teresa of Calcutta: A Biography* (San Francisco: Harper and Row, Publishers, 1983).

Merton, Thomas. *Life and Holiness* (Garden City, NY: Doubleday and Company, Image Books, 1964).

Neff, LaVonne, comp. *A Life for God: The Mother Teresa Reader* (Ann Arbor, MI: Servant Publications, Charis Books, 1995).

Teresa, Mother. *Heart of Joy*. Ed. José Luis González-Balado (Ann Arbor, MI: Servant Books, 1987).

_____. *Jesus, the Word to Be Spoken: Prayers and Meditations for Every Day of the Year.* Comp. Angelo Devananda (Ann Arbor, MI: Servant Books, 1986).

_____. *Life in the Spirit: Reflections, Meditations, Prayers.* Ed. Kathryn Spink (San Francisco: Harper and Row, Publishers, 1983).

_____. *Loving Jesus.* Ed. José Luis González-Balado (Ann Arbor, MI: Servant Publications, 1991).

_____. *My Life for the Poor.* Ed. José Luis González-Balado and Janet N. Playfoot (New York: Ballantine Books, 1985).

_____. *No Greater Love.* Ed. Becky Benenate and Joseph Durepos (Novato, CA: New World Library, 1997).

_____. *One Heart Full of Love.* Ed. José Luis González-Balado (Ann Arbor, MI: Servant Books, 1984).

_____. *A Simple Path.* Comp. Lucinda Vardey (New York: Ballantine Books, 1995).

_____. *Something Beautiful for God.* Ed. Malcolm Muggeridge (Garden City, NY: Doubleday and Company, Image Books, 1977).

# ✧ For Further Reading ✧

Clucas, Joan Graff. *Mother Teresa*. New York: Chelsea House
 Publishers, 1988.

Giff, Patricia Reilly. *Mother Teresa, Sister to the Poor*. New York:
 Puffin Books, 1987.

Gjergji, Lush. *Mother Teresa: Her Life, Her Works*. New York:
 New City Press, 1991.

González-Balado, José Luis. *Mother Teresa: Always the Poor*.
 Liguori, MO: Liguori Publications, 1980.

Ruth, Amy. *Mother Teresa*. Minneapolis: Lerner Publications
 Company, 1999.

Teresa, Mother. *Everything Starts from Prayer: Mother Teresa's
 Meditations on Spiritual Life for People of All Faiths*. Sel. and
 arr. Anthony Stern. Ashland, OR: White Cloud Press, 1998.

———. *The Joy in Loving: A Guide to Daily Living with Mother
 Teresa*. Comp. Jaya Chaliha and Edward Le Joly. New Delhi: Viking, 1996.

**Acknowledgments** *(continued)*

The scriptural quotations contained herein are from the New Revised Standard Version of the Bible. Copyright © 1989 by the Division of Christian Education of the National Council of the Churches of Christ in the United States of America. All rights reserved.

The quotes herein from *A Life for God: The Mother Teresa Reader,* compiled by LaVonne Neff, are used with permission. These quotes are now published under the new title *No Greater Love,* edited by Becky Benenate and Joseph Durepos (Norato, LA: New World Library, 1977). Copyright © 1977 by New World Library.

The quotes herein from *At Prayer with Mother Teresa,* by Eileen Egan, compiled and edited by Judy Bauer, are used by permission of the publisher. Copyright © 1999 by Eileen Egan and Judy Bauer.

The quotes herein from *My Life for the Poor,* by Mother Teresa, edited by José Luis González-Balado and Janet N. Playfoot, are used by permission of the publisher. Copyright © 1995 by José Luis González-Balado and Janet N. Playfoot.

The quotes herein from *Heart of Joy,* by Mother Teresa, edited by José Luis González-Balado, are used by permission of Servant Publications, Box 8617, Ann Arbor, MI 48107. Copyright © 1987 by José Luis González-Balado.

The quotes herein from *Jesus, the Word to Be Spoken: Prayers and Meditations for Every Day of the Year,* by Mother Teresa, compiled by Br. Angelo Devananda, are used by permission. Copyright © 1998 by Servant Publications, Box 8617, Ann Arbor, MI 48107.

The quotes herein from *Life in the Spirit: Reflections, Meditations, Prayers,* by Mother Teresa, edited by Kathryn Spink, are used by permission of Missionaries of Charity. Copyright © by Missionaries of Charity.

The quotes herein from *Mother Teresa: A Woman in Love,* by Edward Le Joly, SJ, are used by permission of the author. Copyright © 1992 by E. Le Joly, SJ.

The quotes herein from *Mother Teresa of Calcutta: A Biography,* by Edward Le Joly, SJ, are used by permission of the publisher. Copyright © 1977, 1983 by Edward Le Joly, SJ.

# Titles in the Companions for the Journey Series

*Praying with Anthony of Padua*
*Praying with Benedict*
*Praying with C. S. Lewis*
*Praying with Catherine McAuley*
*Praying with Catherine of Siena*
*Praying with the Celtic Saints*
*Praying with Clare of Assisi*
*Praying with Dominic*
*Praying with Dorothy Day*
*Praying with Elizabeth Seton*
*Praying with Francis of Assisi*
*Praying with Francis de Sales*
*Praying with Frédéric Ozanam*
*Praying with Hildegard of Bingen*
*Praying with Ignatius of Loyola*
*Praying with John Baptist de La Salle*
*Praying with John Cardinal Newman*
*Praying with John of the Cross*
*Praying with Julian of Norwich*
*Praying with Louise de Marillac*
*Praying with Martin Luther*
*Praying with Meister Eckhart*
*Praying with Mother Teresa*
*Praying with Pope John XXIII*
*Praying with Teresa of Avila*
*Praying with Thérèse of Lisieux*
*Praying with Thomas Aquinas*
*Praying with Thomas Merton*
*Praying with Vincent de Paul*

Order from your local religious bookstore or from

**Saint Mary's Press**
702 TERRACE HEIGHTS
WINONA MN  55987-1320
USA
800-533-8095
www.smp.org